CW00344377

THE WORM-EATEN WAISTCOAT

THE WORM-EATEN WAISTCOAT

Alison Backhouse

To Jenny and Levina

Best Wishes

Alison Backhouse

2003

© Alison Backhouse 2003

First Edition 2003

ISBN 0-9544800-0-7

The right of Alison Backhouse to be identified as author
of this work has been asserted in accordance with
the Copyright, Designs and Patents Act 1988.

Published by
A R Backhouse
4 Elm Tree Avenue
Upper Poppleton
York YO26 6HL

All rights reserved.
No part of this publication may be reproduced or transmitted in any form or by any
means (electronic, mechanical, photocopying, recording or otherwise), or stored in a
database or retrieval system, without the prior written permission of the author.

Cover designs and illustrations by Catherine Hawkes

Printed by J W Bullivant & Son, 296 Bishopthorpe Road, York YO23 1LG

For David
who made me realise
that life was moving on without me

Contents

Acknowledgements

My heartfelt thanks go to Mrs Rita Freedman and her staff at the City of York Archives who have been unfailingly helpful and generous in their encouragement towards me over many years. Rita deserves extra thanks for managing to persuade me to enter the local history essay competition (see below), which had a very surprising outcome, and which consequently spurred me on to greater things. I thank the above-mentioned City of York Archives for granting permission to reproduce the sample page from the pledge book and the other documents found with the book.

I also thank the following:

The Oliver Sheldon Memorial Trust in York who hold an annual essay competition and generously awarded my entry second prize in 1997; the York Architectural and York Archaeological Society for publishing the essay in their magazine *York Historian* Volume 14 (1997), the essay later forming the starting point for this book; the staff at York Reference Library, especially those who first thought of and those who now maintain the excellent newspaper indexes and the many other sources of local history; Josie Sheppard, Curator of Costume, at The Castle Museum, York; Staff at the Merchant Adventurers Hall in Fossgate, York; Staff at the City of York Art Gallery; the Borthwick Institute, University of York, for permission to reproduce documents in their custody; Patricia Mollon for her encouragement and suggestions in the completion of the text; Catherine Hawkes for all the beautiful and very detailed hand-drawn illustrations; Pam Mullen and Linda Haywood for their confidence-building and their belief in me; Mike Brudenell for his expertise with modern technology and the many others who have helped along the way.

The drawings of the two shop signs advertising the Hardcastle business are based on the original signs on view at The Castle Museum, York. The maps preceding chapter 1 are sections from a single map published in 1788 and held by City of York Libraries.

Alison Backhouse
York, 2003

Foreword

I am delighted that the extraordinary and unique pledge book of George Fettes, pawnbroker, has reached publication. I have been aware of its importance as a social record for over thirty years of my tenure here. It only covers the years of 1777-78, but there is so much unexpected information on the customers and the goods they took in.

I still remember the excitement when I first looked at it. The volume urgently needed conservation. It had no cover and the early pages were in tatters and dirty, with significant chunks missing. There were over forty damaged pages with only parts of entries decipherable. The book had presumably been found in the Stonegate/Petergate premises belonging to Henry Reginald Hardcastle, an antique dealer, but it had started its life in Lady Peckett's Yard, Pavement, where George Fettes had his business. Mr Hardcastle deposited it in the Reference Library in York in 1949.

The advent of computers and Alison's expertise with databases led me to suggest that she might be interested in listing the names in it, mainly for family history purposes, and including the street and occupation where present. It soon became evident that this limited version was obviously not going to be satisfactory in view of the detailed information on the items pawned. The decision was made to expand the painstaking work involved and the recording of the complete entries from the book was undertaken by Alison, who entertained us with amusing extracts and observations. From these almost 11,000 entries, the mutual help and cooperation between relatives, friends and neighbours can be seen, where other names redeem items. Occasionally, thieves are exposed by Mr Fettes' meticulous book-keeping, but more often it is unofficial 'borrowing' which has taken place.

What is so important about this pledge book is the insight it gives into the everyday life of the poor, where occasionally even the materials for their trade were pawned, leather and unmade-up gloves for example. Those who had temporarily fallen on difficult times, be they local people or people passing through the city for race meetings, had need of the pawnbroker's service and even the landed gentry are represented.

The volume gives an enormous amount of information on the items pawned, mainly clothes, but also tools of the trade, household items, occasional books or Bibles and valuables including silver (the marks are noted) and watches (the manufacturer and serial number is nearly always given). This efficient and very active business must have been representative of many such enterprises all over the country, but this volume appears to be the only one surviving from the eighteenth century.

The Worm-Eaten Waistcoat is the first book to chart the history of a vital service to the community starting with a day-to-day account of over two hundred years ago. There is a wealth of fascinating information to suit both the serious researcher and to entertain the casual reader. I hope that this book achieves the circulation it deserves and I wish this enterprise well.

Rita Freedman, City Archivist
February 2003

Preface

Firstly, a few remarks which do not fit easily into the main text.

- Lady *Peckett's* Yard or Lady *Peckitt's* Yard?

Controversy has surrounded the spelling of the name of this narrow alley for many, many years. It started as *Peckett* with an *e* in the early eighteenth century, but by the middle of the nineteenth century, the name was spelled as *Peckitt* with an *i*. One hundred years later, it had reverted to *Peckett*. York's own local newspaper, *The Yorkshire Evening Press*, investigated the alley's history in 1977 and concluded that *Peckett* was correct. Four years later, the York Tourist Development Association presented a plaque to the City with the name spelled again as *Peckitt*. The City Council disagreed with them and the new name sign showed *Peckett*. No doubt the debate is not yet at an end.

In the text of this book, the spelling has been standardised on Peckett with an *e*. The only exceptions are the illustration facing the start of Chapter 6 and the large newspaper advertisement in the same chapter, which are reproduced with the *i*, as in the originals.

- The surname Fettes should be pronounced to rhyme with Betty's.

- The people of York who visited the pawnbroker in Lady Peckett's Yard surely never expected to be remembered and written about in the twenty-first century. I hope they would approve of their treatment here but if not, I offer them my apologies. If a reader recognises one of their ancestors within the following pages, the author would very much enjoy hearing from him or her.

- City of York Archives (CYA) may be contacted as follows:

Opening hours:	Monday to Friday, 9.00 to 12.50, 14.00 to 16.50
Address:	City of York Archives, Exhibition Square, York YO1 7EW
Telephone:	01904-551878
e-mail:	archives@york.gov.uk

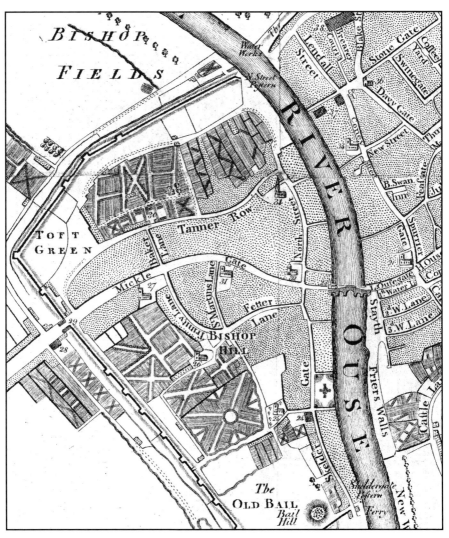

Western York – From 'A Plan of the City of York' by Mr F Consitt, 1788
(Courtesy of City of York Libraries)

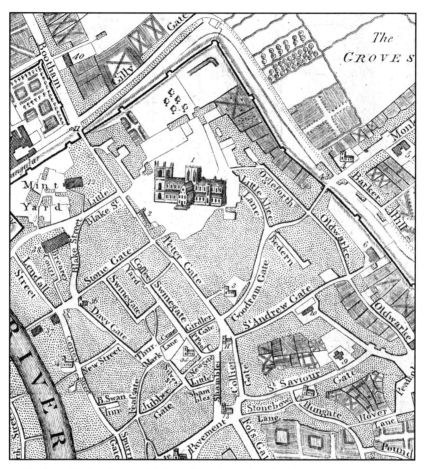

Northern York – From 'A Plan of the City of York' by Mr F Consitt, 1788
(Courtesy of City of York Libraries)

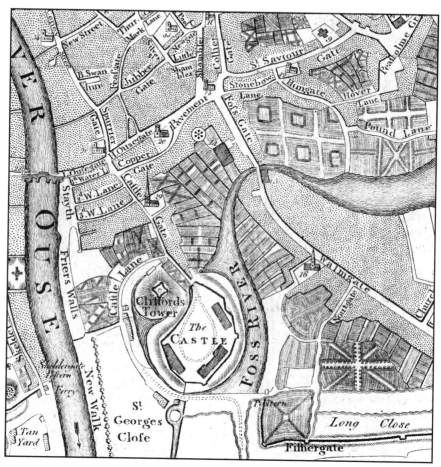

Southern York – From 'A Plan of the City of York' by Mr F Consitt, 1788
(Courtesy of City of York Libraries)

Lady Peckett's Yard connects Pavement with Fossgate (marked with * on the map)

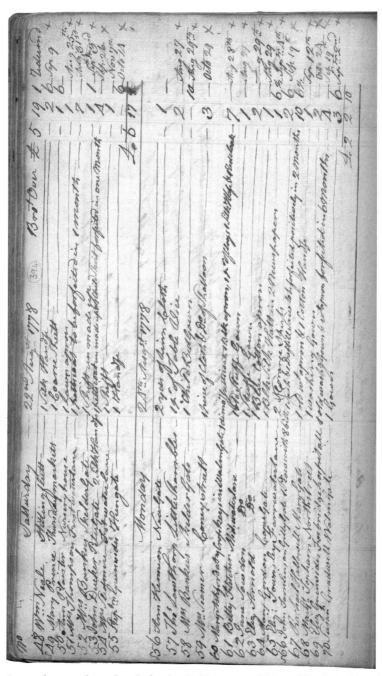

A sample page from the pledge book (Courtesy of City of York Archives)

1

Early Beginnings

'Go West, Young Man!' was the exhortation to the youth of North America in the nineteenth century. One hundred years earlier, the cry which George Fettes heard in Edinburgh was 'Go South, Young Man!' and he did just that. By the late 1770s, he had travelled 200 miles south and was working in the pawnbroker's shop in Lady Peckett's Yard in York.

The trade of the pawnbroker has long been an essential part of every-day life for many people and it remains so to this day. Personal items (the pledges) are left with the pawnbroker in exchange for cash. The owner of the pledge agrees to pay a rate of interest on the sum advanced and will receive the goods back when the loan has been repaid, plus the interest. If the borrower (the customer) defaults, the lender (the pawnbroker) has the right to sell the goods to recover his costs.

Throughout history, pawnbrokers have helped the inhabitants of their locality, but they were not necessarily the first port of call by the needy as the gap between their earnings and spending widened. People requiring money generally had five choices from whom they might borrow:

- friends and families, where possible
- shop-keepers and retailers, who kept their own notes of debtors
- pawnbrokers, for small sums
- banks and mortgage lenders, for large sums
- or loan sharks, if all else failed.

Yet the pawn shops provided an important service for not only the poor and hungry – King Edward III of England is said to have been counted amongst their customers during the fourteenth century, when he pledged his crown on three separate occasions. In 1339 he pledged the queen's crown as well, followed soon after by the crown jewels. In the following century, Queen Isabella of Spain pawned her royal jewels to enable Christopher Columbus to set out on his long voyage of discovery to the New World.

Many pawnbrokers were Jewish and with good reason. Following the destruction of Jerusalem in 70AD, the Jews were forced to leave their own country and disperse to wherever they could find refuge from bitter persecution. They began to settle in England after the Norman Conquest and, due to their hard-working nature, they prospered, causing envy in some of the other merchants. In the wake of the First Crusade (1096-99), Jews were forbidden to enter the guilds which controlled trade and crafts and so were unable to operate as merchants. The Old Testament (the Jewish Bible) prohibited Jews from usury (money-lending for interest) but only towards fellow Jews: lending to a foreigner was acceptable. The Christian Church of the New Testament also had laws against usury, leaving that risky business as the only profitable source of revenue open to the Jews. As a way of lessening the risk to themselves, they asked for something to be left with them as a surety for the loan.

By the fifteenth century, the Church had forbidden Christians in Northern Europe to take part in money-lending for profit, but the practice was allowed in Italy and a number of respectable Christian banking firms existed. Franciscan monks in Perousa, Italy, established the 'monts-de-piété' or 'Banks of Pity' in 1462 to enable struggling people to obtain small loans on presentation of some item as security. They were in opposition to the powerful Medici family of Florence, whose family motto was 'Money to get power, power to protect money'. Legend has it that one of the Medici family had fought a giant and slew him with three sacks of rocks, so naturally three sacks or balls became part of their family crest.

The Medicis controlled a powerful trading and banking empire and their consciences were not troubled by the trade of the pawnbroker. Indeed, one of their family was elected as Pope Leo X in 1513 and he declared that the pawnshop was a lawful and valuable institution and threatened with excommunication anyone who presumed to express doubts on the subject – little sign of religious protection there, despite the Bible stating 'it is illegal to take a millstone as a pledge, for it is a tool by which its owner gains his livelihood' and 'never accept a widow's garment in pledge of her debt'.[1] The family were so well-known amongst bankers and moneylenders that other traders wanted to share in their success, hence the Medici coat of arms was widely copied with only slight variations. Three golden balls was the most popular reproduction and eventually became the sign of a pawnbroker by association with that family.

Another, and much earlier, explanation of the symbol of pawnbrokers takes a more praiseworthy approach. The patron Saint of pawnbrokers is Saint Nicholas of Myra, an ancient city in Turkey. He died c350AD and pictures of Saint Nicholas often show him next to three bags of gold, or three balls or discs – reflecting a legend that he gave three bags of gold anonymously to a man with three unmarried daughters, so that each girl had enough money for a dowry and so could marry instead of having to support themselves by prostitution. Another legend describes how he raised enough money to pay off kidnappers who were holding to ransom most of the children of Myra – the ransom was paid in the form of three bags of gold. Yet another legend has him reviving three children who had been killed, then preserved in a tub of brine. He was reputed to have performed many good deeds, including rescues of desperate, storm-tossed sailors.

Just as Saint Nicholas was a friend to the poor and helpless, pawnbrokers may also have thought of themselves in the same way and, as a means of associating themselves with him, they adopted his already well-known symbol of three golden balls. Saint Nicholas is also the patron Saint of bankers, seafarers, marriageable young women, Russians and especially children and he was probably the original Santa Claus or Father Christmas.

Whether the sign of the three balls derives its origins from giant-killing or from an act of compassion, or even from a completely different escapade, we shall never know for certain.

Pawnbroking is said to date back at least 3,000 years in China, but it was abolished there in 1949 when the People's Republic of China was founded. However, as pawnshops had formerly been so lucrative for their owners, the state permitted such shops to trade again from the 1980s, this time under the control of China's central bank, to serve individuals and private businesses and to grant small loans.

Some of us may have grown up with the idea that using a pawnbroker was a rather shameful thing to do, and Charles Dickens must bear much of the responsibility for this impression. He lived from 1812 to 1870 and worked his way up from very humble origins to become one of England's most famous writers. Many of his works contain references to pawnbrokers – *Pickwick Papers, Oliver Twist, A Christmas Carol, Little Dorrit,* to name a few. As a journalist, under the pen name Boz, he wrote gripping accounts exposing social conditions in England. In one of his articles entitled *The Pawnbroker's Shop,* he powerfully described his observations of such an establishment, beginning by calling it a 'receptacle for misery and distress' and going on to describe the shop, its unhappy customers and their meagre items for pledge. In *The Mystery of Edwin Drood,* he uses the description of a pawnbroker to describe the atmosphere of the cathedral town of Cloisterham:

> All things in it [Cloisterham] are of the past. Even its single pawnbroker takes in no pledges, nor has he for a long time, but offers vainly an unredeemed stock for sale, of which the costlier articles are dim and pale old watches apparently in a slow perspiration, tarnished sugar-tongs with ineffectual legs, and odd volumes of dismal books.

The following extract from *Nicholas Nickleby* shows how the poor felt about pawnbrokers, describing with glee how Arthur, for once, got the better of one of them:

> 'The bottle-green,' said old Arthur; 'the bottle-green was a famous suit to wear, and I bought it very cheap at a pawnbroker's, and there was – he, he, he! – a tarnished shilling in the waistcoat pocket. To think that the pawnbroker shouldn't have known there was a shilling in it! I knew it! I felt it when I was examining the quality. Oh, what a dull dog of a pawnbroker!'

In *Martin Chuzzlewit,* Dickens gives a vivid illustration of what it was like to approach and enter the pawnbroker's territory:

...it was growing dusk again. This was all the better, for it was now a matter of absolute necessity that he should part with his watch to some obliging pawnbroker. He would have waited until after dark for this purpose, though it had been the longest day in the year, and he had begun it without a breakfast.

He passed more Golden Balls than all the jugglers in Europe have juggled with in the course of their united performances, before he could determine in favour of any particular shop where those symbols were displayed. In the end he came back to one of the first he had seen, and entering by a side-door in a court, where the three balls, with the legend 'Money Lent,' were repeated in a ghastly transparency, [he] passed into one of a series of little closets, or private boxes, erected for the accommodation of the more bashful and uninitiated customers. He bolted himself in; pulled out his watch; and laid it on the counter.

It was not only Dickens who described pawnbrokers in a derogatory manner. In 1751, the English artist William Hogarth (1697 - 1764) depicted what he called 'the dreadful consequences of gin-drinking' in his picture *Gin Lane*, of which he wrote:

In Gin Lane, every circumstance of its horrid effects is brought to view *in terrorem*. Idleness, poverty, misery, and distress which drives even to madness and death, are the only objects that are to be seen; and not a house in tolerable condition but the pawnbroker's and the gin shop.

The Russian author Anton Chekhov (1860 - 1904) certainly knew how to use a pawnbroker, for in his book *A Gentleman Friend* he writes:

[she was] in a position she had never been in before: without a home to go to or a farthing in her pocket. What was she to do? The first thing she did was to visit a pawnbroker's and pawn her turquoise ring, her one piece of jewellery.

The founder of The Salvation Army (and former Methodist minister) William Booth worked as a pawnbroker's clerk when he left school in the 1840s and he was so appalled at the deprivation and misery he saw that he determined to do something about it.

However, pawnbroking was not always viewed in such a negative light. Pawnshops were legal, as well as being quick, convenient and non-judgemental, and they no doubt helped to reduce the number of thefts by people with an urgent need for cash. The Methodist leader John Wesley lodged at George Fettes' house in Lady Peckett's Yard several times on his journeys to York in the eighteenth century – it is hard to imagine him being so friendly with the pawnbroker if he considered him to be in any way immoral or dishonest, or whose actions were in contradiction to his own firm beliefs.

It may be worth drawing the reader's attention at this point to some of the appendices, which may be useful in giving a better understanding of what follows. Appendix A lists the items which were pledged in the York shop during 1777 and 1778 and how frequently each type of item was deposited. Appendices E, F and G describe some of the possibly unfamiliar terms used in the eighteenth century and Appendix I gives a brief explanation of the currency of the time.

The entrance to Lady Peckett's Yard from Pavement

2

The Pledge Book

Among the countless treasures kept by the City of York Archives is a pledge book from an eighteenth century pawnbroker's business in the centre of old York. The pledge book was the daily record of the customers who visited the pawn shop in Lady Peckett's Yard during 1777 and 1778, what they pawned, how much money they received and whether or not they reclaimed their goods and chattels. It was nothing very remarkable at all at that time, yet viewed through the eyes of the twenty-first century, this single volume becomes a witness to a bygone time and guards numerous mysteries which can never be fully explained.

The pawnbroker responsible for keeping the pledge book was George Fettes, the young man who had ventured south from Edinburgh in the 1770s. Lady Peckett's Yard was more than a small open space behind a street, which we today might think of as a yard – it was indeed a yard, but the location included not only the long narrow alley or lane which connected it with the main thoroughfare called Pavement but also the shorter alley at a right-angle to it which led into Fossgate (see the map on page 13). In former times, the two lanes were known respectively as Bacus gail (Bake-house Lane) and Trichour gail (Cheat's Lane).[2]

Lady Peckett's Yard would not have been the most noticeable thoroughfare to a person unfamiliar with the City of York and it was such a narrow alley that Mr Consitt deemed it too insignificant to include when he compiled his map of the city in 1788. However, the alley was in a prime trading position – it was very close to the intersection of roads leading from the only two river crossings in the city, it had an entrance in not one but two popular thoroughfares, and, in addition, Pavement was the site of a frequent market. All these factors would have ensured a continuous flow of potential customers in the vicinity. The alley is believed to have been named after Lady Alice Peckett, wife of a one-time Lord Mayor of York who lived in Pavement, and it is still there to this day, bearing the same name, but its central yard has been much reduced in size due to being built on.

The pawnbroker's pledge book gives a wonderful insight into the private lives of several hundred citizens of York and is bursting with information not usually available to researchers and historians. From it, one can learn specific details of the clothes which the customers and their families wore. Furnishings for their homes were listed, along with household utensils. A number of items were brought into the shop on behalf of other people, showing that the customers and the goods' owners were at least acquainted and possibly good friends. Some people had their occupation noted or their employer or even their regiment. Some gave their address at a local lodging house or hotel, or occasionally the city jail, and yet others were from a different town or city, proving that on a certain day those people were not at home but in York.

This fascinating book measures 13" by 8" by 1¾" (33.3 cm by 20.4 cm by 4.7 cm). It was restored about thirty years ago and is now in very good condition, except for forty-four damaged pages near the beginning where the originals have pieces missing. There are a total of 494 pages, each ruled by the printer into eight columns, and containing almost 11,000 entries. The earliest pledge recorded was for 5 July 1777 and the final entry was for 26 December 1778. After each day, the value of pledges for the day was totalled, then the day and date of the next day's trading were written right across the page on the next line. The entries were written by about six different hands and all are remarkably readable.

This small round label removed from the back cover of the pledge book during restoration and bearing the words 'Grimshaw Dringhouses' may indicate the printer.

The eight columns ruled in the pledge book were used as follows.

1. **Entry number**. This generally runs from 1 to 100 and then starts again at 1. However, a significant proportion of numbers appear out of sequence and some are repeated on consecutive lines although not necessarily for the same customer.
2. The **name** of the person said to be the owner of the goods pledged.
3. The **abode** of the said owner. These last two columns may also hold the name and abode of the customer if they have brought goods on behalf of someone else.
4. The **description of the goods** brought for pawn, along with any special conditions which apply such as a forfeit date, and sometimes a comment about the transaction.
5. The money advanced for the goods in **pounds** (£).
6. The money advanced for the goods in **shillings** (s).
7. The money advanced for the goods in **pence** (d).
8. The **date the goods were redeemed**, or blank for unclaimed items. Occasionally this column contains 'sold' and a date and/or value.

The monetary value, in columns 5, 6 and 7, should not be thought of as the value of the goods as though they were being sold, for two reasons. Firstly, many customers only wanted the cash to tide them over for a while and it would cost them less in interest when they came to redeem their pledges if they had accepted only the sum immediately necessary. Having said that, if they never intended to redeem a pledge, it was certainly in their best interests to try to prise as much as possible from the pawnbroker's cash box when their goods were deposited. Secondly, the pawnbroker himself would have been extremely averse to handing over more cash than he thought he would be able to sell an item for in case he got left with it.

When I was first shown the pledge book, my idea was merely to compile an index of the names in it using a computer, so that the individual names could be located more easily and hence assist people who were engaged in the popular pursuit of tracing their family history. However, this soon changed as the details of the book became more and more engrossing: regular customers kept appearing, often with the same items for pledge, some streets of York supplied many more customers than did other streets, customers came from other areas of the country, many unusual items were brought in, tantalising comments were recorded about some customers, and just who were those people who had written and kept the book so carefully?

It was soon apparent that a mere index would not satisfy my curiosity, but at the same time a rather daunting task seemed to be suggesting itself – could I type in *all* the information held in the pledge book and, no less significant, how long would it take? Given that I was working on it for only half a day per week, there were 494 pages, most were closely written and at a rate of typing of about three to four pages per week … the answer came to several years! I resolved to make a start and see how far I could get.

Having taken the decision to record all the information from the pledge book, it was then decided that the information might be capable of more thorough analysis if the goods pawned were entered into appropriate columns on the computer depending on the type of item pawned, rather than being in a single column as they were in the book. Consequently, the computer database was designed to hold the information in the following twenty-two fields.

1. The City of York Archives internal reference number.
2. The date the goods were pledged.
3. The entry number.
4. The day of the week of the pledge.
5. The surname of the owner of the pledge.
6. The other names of the owner.
7. The modern spelling or modern location of the owner's abode.
8. The abode of the owner as written in the pledge book.
9. The name and abode of the person who brought the goods for pawn, if not the owner.
10. Clothing worn by adults.
11. Clothing worn by children.

12. Hats, caps, bonnets, wigs, shoes, boots.
13. Handkerchiefs.
14. Household goods, including silverware, tradesman's tools, books.
15. Jewellery, including watches, buttons, buckles.
16. Other items, which was mostly used for entries which were only partially readable.
17. Number of pounds given for the pledge.
18. Number of shillings given for the pledge.
19. Number of pence given for the pledge.
20. Any specified forfeit conditions.
21. The date when the pledge was redeemed.
22. Comments, to record other details about the transaction such as occupations, etc.

Eventually(!), all 10,900+ entries were input to the computer database, thereby allowing the information to be sorted and analysed in many different ways. The original spellings in the pledge book were retained in the database, but in order to make this account more readable, some spellings have been modernised where necessary. For example: hatt, checkt, plaited, sleives (as written in the book) have been replaced by their modern spellings of hat, checked, plated, sleeves and abbreviations such as blk and hkffe replaced by black and handkerchief.

Throughout the pledge book, whenever there is a redemption date written against a pledge there is an 'x' marked against it, and all the pledges which were *not* redeemed have an 's' written next to their entry. This suggests that information from the book regarding redemptions was being transferred into another ledger at the end of each month and being marked with an 'x' when it had been copied, possibly to show the pawnbroker how much money had been received each month from redeemed pledges (but it did not show the amount of interest). The 's' suggests that the unredeemed pledges were being copied into yet another book, possibly into a catalogue of sale. The only exceptions are all the pledges deposited during December 1778, the final (and incomplete) month of the book. As the end of December 1778 had not yet occurred, the end-of-month procedures were not due, hence no 'x's against the redeemed pledges.

The completed database, along with the restored pledge book, is available for consultation at City of York Archives. Details of how to contact the Archives can be found in the Preface.

3

The Customers and Their Pledges

The customers visiting George Fettes' pledge office in Lady Peckett's Yard came mainly from the centre of York, but not exclusively. Some regulars were from Clifton, Dunnington, Heslington and Fulford on the outskirts of the City and there were occasional callers from much further afield. The vast majority of the goods they pledged (75%) were items of clothing worn by adults – these were their principal, if not their only, assets. People were usually pawning the necessities of life, not the luxuries. There were many gowns, aprons, cloaks, coats and waistcoats and a surprising number of pairs of stays, even leather stays. Almost 10% of all pledges were described as 'old'. On seventeen occasions, the pledge was merely a pair of buttons.

Customers often pawned more than one item at a time, but they also pawned single items. The twelve most frequent *single* pledges, exactly as described in the pledge book, are shown below – but be aware that if a pledge was recorded as, for example, '1 old cotton gown' rather than '1 cotton gown', it is not counted in this table.

Single Item	Number of Times Pledged	Not Redeemed	
		Number of Times	Percentage of Pledges
Checked apron	344	37	11
Cotton gown	330	57	17
Coat	191	24	13
Shirt	155	21	14
Silk handkerchief	142	23	16
Washing gown	127	20	16
Waistcoat	118	24	20
Linen gown	115	25	22
Red or scarlet cloak	106	17	16
Pair of leather breeches	102	7	7
Coat and waistcoat	101	14	14
Gold ring	96	27	28

The final two columns show how many of the single pledges were not redeemed and what percentage they represent of those single pledges. Single items may reflect the haste in which the customer set off for the pawnbroker's shop, not having the time to choose several things to take for pawn, or perhaps the customer only needed the money which a single item would earn, or maybe even it was all the customer could spare from what remained of his/her meagre possessions. The most disquieting value in the above table is the percentage of gold rings which were unredeemed – 28% of the single pledges, which surely reflects the haste or the desperation, for they were probably the owners' wedding rings.

For a complete list of all the items pledged, whether singly or not, please refer to Appendix A.

Adult Clothing

The very first customer on the morning of Wednesday 14 October 1778 was Samuel Robinson from the nearby street of Walmgate. He had brought his waistcoat. One might well imagine the joy of the pawnbroker on inspecting it, for he wrote in his register 'one waistcoat but on account of its being worm-eaten must be forfeited if not redeemed in one month' – possibly the worms were still alive and well! It was unclaimed, so Samuel had sold what remained of his waistcoat for 1s-0d.

John Burniston from near Tadcaster sent his coat and waistcoat to finance his marriage. The note on 2 August 1777 reads 'Brought by his mother Mary Cousens, who lives in ye Great Shambles up Fawcett's yard, said her son lives in a farmers place in the country near Tadcaster and is going to be married [but] could not draw any money on his master, which obliged him to send this coat & waistcoat to her last night by his brother for her to pledge for him'. The sum raised was 16s-0d and John probably intended to redeem the coat and waistcoat before the winter weather set in, but as it turned out, he had to rely on his love to keep him warm during those dark, cold days for he did not redeem his clothing for a whole eight months, finally reclaiming it on 2 April 1778.

The pawnbroker would have been well acquainted with his regular customers. Mrs Riley of North Street pawned a shirt on fifty-six occasions, Mary Metcalfe of Walmgate pledged gloves twenty-five times, Mary Budd of Thursday Market pledged four gowns, two black satin cloaks, one velvet cloak, one coat and waistcoat, one pair of ruffles, four women's waistcoats, one child jam (a type of frock), one child's petticoat and a shift each month for ten consecutive months. John Thompson of First Water Lane pawned his leather breeches on thirty-one occasions, twenty-three of them being for five days or fewer, and usually on a Monday.

Aron Martin, staying at The Three Cranes in Girdlergate, pledged a complete gentleman's outfit in June 1778 – namely a suit of clothes, a pair of shoes and one hat – for £1-1s-0d and reclaimed them three weeks later. If he was not a travelling salesman pawning his samples, did his wife enquire where his clothes were when he returned home, sending him back to fetch them as soon as money was available? Or, more likely, he had pawned his Sunday best and had to endure the disapproving comments of his neighbours at church until he could afford to wear them again.

Occasionally, the pawnbroker was offered well-made clothing as pledges. Ann Nickleson of Walmgate pawned her very best clothes and they must have been of excellent quality, for they were recorded as 'one good satin cloak, one new cotton gown, one pair of good stays and a bit of cotton' for £1-11s-0d.[3] None were redeemed.

On 21 February 1778, Richard Blackburne of Petergate pawned only parts of his waistcoat, namely a pair of waistcoat sleeves and twelve waistcoat buttons (plus twenty-three coat buttons) for 8d.[4] Some waistcoats had sleeves which could be attached for warmth during the winter and detached again during warmer weather. Astonishingly, items which were only partly made were a fairly common pledge; for example, one shift un made up,[5] one pair of sleeves un made up,[6] one black quilted petticoat un made up,[7] one scarlet gown all in pieces,[8] one coarse apron un made.[9] Several of the articles were probably undergoing alterations or repairs and, as the money was needed without delay, these were the things which the families could most readily manage without for a while.

The greatest number of items partly made was pledged by Mary Metcalfe of Walmgate. She was a frequent customer, often visiting the shop several times a week and sometimes several times a day. She brought in up to six pairs of gloves at a time, usually described as 'un made up', but on 12 September 1777 she pledged six pairs of gloves *made* for 7s-0d. The pawnbroker was so surprised to see some gloves from her which were ready to wear that he commented on the fact in the register – and he had plenty of time to recover from the shock because they were never redeemed.

During the second half of the eighteenth century, a handkerchief was not used for the same purpose as it is today. It was not a small piece of cloth used to dry a runny nose, but was the most common form of neck covering worn by women. In the 1770s, handkerchiefs were large and draped round the neck and shoulders, rather like a shawl, and were often secured with a pin or brooch (if the wearer owned one). They were a frequent pledge (12%) and many were noted as being made of silk (28%) or cotton (7%) and were often black (14%).

In Chapter 2, Mr Consitt was mentioned as the man who drew the map of York in 1788, but who failed to include Lady Peckett's Yard. He may have deliberately left it out, possibly following some (in his opinion) unsatisfactory dealings by one of his relatives with Mr Fettes. A William Consitt of Walmgate visited the pawn shop five times towards the end of 1778 – he pledged a quilted petticoat and a washing gown which were unredeemed, and twice pawned a coat which he did redeem. By Christmas Eve, he was in very dire straights, for he pawned his hat and his Bible for 6d. We shall never know if he redeemed them or not, since the pledge book was not used after 26 December.

Children's Clothing

Children were usually dressed in smaller versions of adult clothing in the eighteenth century and nearly 6% of the pledges (628 entries) included items worn by children. Of those pledges, 503 were redeemed (80% of them), greater than the usual rate for redemptions.

Bearing in mind that clothes for a child would often have been cut down from adult clothing, if a child's item was described as 'old', it was probably extremely old and well-worn. 'One boys coat, very old' pledged by William Addey of Holgate Lane for 6d could well have been threadbare and falling to bits.[10] 'Two very bad child flannel petticoats' from Rachael Hallowell of Marygate presumably refers to the condition of the petticoats rather than the mental state of the child who wore them.[11] Hannah Harrison of Walmgate had a clearout of her family's attire, for she pledged ten child caps, six bibs, three child shirts, four hippings, two child night gowns, a barrow, a child petticoat and a shift for 3s-0d on 4 October 1777 and redeemed them eleven days later. Katty Cundill of North Street pledged her child's vest five times, usually for 1s-0d. Mrs Martin of Swinegate pledged her daughter's stuff gown every week without fail from 30 December 1777 to 28 March 1778, usually for 1s-6d, only permitting the girl to wear it on a Sunday.

The following table shows a sample of items which were specifically noted as worn by boys, girls or children. Remember, a pledge may consist of more than one item. The only unwearable items pawned which belonged to children were two pin-cushions, one each by Joseph Poplewell and Jane Rothwell, both of Skeldergate.

Child's Item	Number of Times Pledged
Frock	155
Gown	142
Skirt	68
Coat	50
Shirt	49
Jam	45
Petticoat	35
Cap	34
Waistcoat	26
Shift	19
Apron	17
Lapper	13
Breeches	12
Hat	11
Stockings	9
Cloak	9
Shoes	8
Stays	5

Headwear

Wigs became less fashionable as the end of the century approached, but they were still relatively popular in York – wigs were pledged twelve times and the majority of them were redeemed. John Nailer of North Street wore his wig at the weekend, for he brought it in only on a Tuesday or Wednesday and redeemed it the following Saturday. He liked to look his best on a Sunday for, as well as his wig, he regularly pawned his black coat and waistcoat at the beginning of a week and redeemed them the following Saturday. The other wigs belonged to James Richardson of Pavement and Derby, Richard Beeforth of Shambles, John Tate of Goodramgate, who kept his wig in a box, and Christopher Sellers of Fossgate.

Katty Cundill of North Street pawned her cap (worn indoors) for 1s-0d just before Christmas 1777. Despite being fancy and elaborate, the cap was far from looking its best and she was told to come back for it before Easter, which she did. It was described as 'one dressed up cap but as it has been thrown into ye dirt [it is] to be forfeited in three months'. Mary Scot of Peter Lane[12] and Bella Richardson of North Street Church Yard[13] both took much greater care of their silk hats (worn outdoors), for they pledged them complete with hat boxes. Ann Mason of Micklegate also owned a hat box but apparently no hat, for she pledged a bolster inside hers.[14]

Footwear

One hundred and forty pairs of shoes, twenty pairs of boots, one pair of boot legs and one pair of boot garters were pledged. Thomas Frude of Petergate owned three pairs of boots for he twice pledged and redeemed them all at once in the summer of 1778. Mrs Moore of Girdlergate worked on her unmade shoes whenever she had a few hours to spare. During February 1778, she pledged unmade shoes seven times but usually redeemed them within four days and pledged them again soon afterwards.

Martha Wilson of Micklegate pledged a pair of shoes fourteen times and always redeemed them on a Saturday. The Beeforth family of Shambles (Richard, Betty and Sarah) were shoe makers, pledging their shoe-making equipment as well as their shoes and their partly made clogs.

Occupations

Several items listed in the pledge book suggest how the customers may have made their living. The afore-mentioned Mary Metcalfe of Walmgate probably made gloves, when she got round to it, and the Beeforth family were shoe-makers. During five weeks in July and August 1777, Isabella Brown of Walmgate Bar appeared to be making tea trays for she pledged six of them, including three of mahogany, on five visits to the pawnbroker and never redeemed any of them.

Name	Address	Occupation
Richard Baker	Goodramgate	Joiner
Joseph Balgey	Army	Corporal in the 36 Reg't of foot
John Benson	Shambles	Baker
Mr Benson	Goodramgate	Tallow chandler
Ann Bouls	Fossgate	Hickson's maid servant
Ralph Bristall	none	Servant to Mrs Wolfe
Robert Brown	Stonegate	Tailor
George Butter	Sheffield	Button maker
Alice Cary's brother	Walmgate	Joiner
Matthew Dilman	Skeldergate	Trumpeter
Ann Hayes	none	Travelling woman
Mr Johnson	Fossgate	Dyer
Mr Johnson	Goodramgate	Painter
Mary Mills	Walmgate	A dragoon wife
Nickson Senr	Bishophill	Tailor
Joseph Pamplin	Army	Trumpeter 11th Regiment
John Phipson	Feasegate	Pipemaker
Anthony Pitts	none	Mr Willbor's cutter-out
William Potter	Minster Yard	A gentleman servant
Wm Sanderson	none	Tinplate worker
Thomas Savage	none	Boatman at the Butter Staith
Joseph Smith	Coney Street	Quack doctor
John Sunter	none	William Bradley's apprentice
J Swinbank	none	Castlegate overseer
Richard Thompson	Knaresborough	Mr Stockdill's clerk
James Walker	Low Petergate	Shoemaker
William Walker	Maison Dieu	Bricklayer labourer
Mr Warren	Aldwark	Pensioner
Mary Webster	none	The deaf woman
Joseph Young	Army	Corporal in Johnston's Dragoons
Matthew Young	Spurriergate	Shoemaker

Some of the occupations and descriptions of customers noted in the pledge book

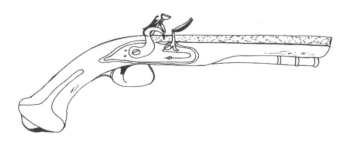

On 21 August 1777, Leonard Camidge of Coney Street brought in one case of drawing tools for 6s-0d which remained unredeemed. In the space of three weeks from 28 August 1777, William Brown of Grape Lane brought in one pair of planes, two planes, and ten planes, for which he received a total of 8s-6d. None were redeemed which leaves one wondering how such people could have made a living without them.

In contrast, the Scrivin family of Middle Water Lane (John, Mrs and Ann) pledged four saws and twenty-three planes during March 1778 for a total of £1-2s-10d. They redeemed all of them on 8 May 1778, which poses the questions: why they would need twenty-three planes and how could Mr Scrivin manage without any of them during the whole of April?

When Joseph Smith of Coney Street pledged his pinchbeck watch for the second time, the pawnbroker noted that he was a 'quack doctor' – and presumably not a particularly popular one with his clients, or else he would not have been so short of cash as to be obliged to visit a pawnbroker.[15]

Household Items

Think of any item in the home of an eighteenth century citizen of York – whether wealthy or not – and you would probably have found one of those items at some time in the pawnbroker's warehouse. Curtains, carpets, candlesticks, crockery, chairs, clocks, linen, beds, pictures, artificial flowers, garden sheers … the list was almost endless. All these, and more, went to and fro between home and the pledge shop.

During the winter, Mrs Bower of Peter Lane usually did her ironing at the weekend – she pledged a flat iron midweek and redeemed it the following Saturday on thirteen occasions between October 1777 and March 1778. Eliz Harrison of Feasegate pledged two unwanted window curtains for 1s-6d[16] and Mrs Brown of Goodramgate pawned a carpet for 5s-0d and returned for it eleven weeks later.[17]

Alice Cary of Walmgate visited the pawnbroker thirty-three times during twelve weeks from November 1777, usually pledging clothing or bedding. Later, on 16 April 1778, she pawned an iron fender for 1s-9d which was redeemed by her brother's wife 'to buy Alice some necessaries' on 19 May. Unfortunately, we have to imagine what these 'necessaries' might have been. Yet here is her sister-in-law paying money to the pawnbroker so that she could buy essentials – did she have a buyer for the iron fender which would produce more money than would have been saved in interest and capital? On the same day, her sister-in-law also redeemed Alice's copper jug for her. These acts of kindness apparently sorted out Alice's finances for the time being, for she had no need to pledge any more goods for five months.

Edward Milner from Tadcaster caught up with his spring-cleaning in May 1778, pledging the contents of his bedroom for 14s-0d – namely, one old bed, three old blankets, three old pillows but one of them chaff (meaning that it was made of hay or straw rather than of feathers), three old curtains and one old quilt – and redeemed them three weeks later.[18]

On 24 January 1778, in the depths of winter, Betty Bridgewater travelled about 20 miles south from Kilburn to York with a feather bed, bolster and bed quilt, receiving £1-8s-0d. Six days later, she arrived with a counterpane described as 'very much worm-eaten', received 2s-6d and agreed to reclaim it within three months. It languished in the pawnbroker's warehouse for almost three months, until on 23 April she re-pawned it, again for 2s-6d, this time with no time limit. Four months later, on 27 August, she re-pawned it again for the same sum, with a two month time limit, but now it is described as 'much damaged'. It may have been the recipient of some rough handling during its seven months of storage, or the comment could indicate that the worms were flourishing, or possibly both. She must have decided that the counterpane was not worth having because it was not redeemed again – neither were the feather bed, the bolster, nor the bed quilt.

Benjamin Burkhead, staying at the Royal Oak in Thursday Market in August and September 1777, first brought in one dog skin and a piece of calves skin for 2s-0d.[19] He returned for them two days later on the following Saturday, but by Tuesday the dog skin was back again along with one handkerchief for 1s-6d. On Friday he redeemed these two items and pawned instead a pair of boots for 10s-6d. Two weeks later he was back in the shop for the last time, but not to collect his boots – he reported that he had transferred them to Daniel Chapell, who promptly sold them to the pawnbroker for an additional 1s-6d – it would seem that the pawnbroker had, by then, discovered that they fitted his own feet rather well.

Thomas Simpson journeyed from Heslington three times in one week in November 1778 to pawn two knives and forks on a Monday, another knife and fork the next day, and finally a hand bell on the Saturday. He received the grand sum of only 1s-2d for his efforts and was not seen in the shop again.

Thomas Gowland Esquire of Poppleton was in York on 29 and 30 September 1778. He pledged a pair of stays, two gowns, a petticoat, a tablecloth, a silver cup engraved with G T M, eleven silver teaspoons engraved M G, a spoon engraved W T D, nine pairs of sheets, two quilts, two pairs of blankets and a set of bed hangings for a total of £8-8s-0d. The pawnbroker was pleased to receive that sum plus interest when Thomas returned for everything on 23 November.

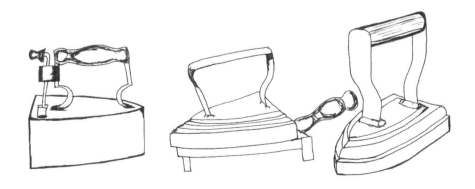

Books were few and far between for the working classes in the eighteenth century. Although some people could write their name, many were unable to read, so a book may have been less useful to them than the money. The books which were offered as pledges usually secured small loans of less than 2s-0d and one wonders how they had been acquired. On 11 December 1777, Jane Newcombe of Fossgate pawned 'one old book, history of Scotland' which she did not want – what value this might have today? Also pawned, by various people, were prayer books, a hymn book and several Bibles. An English dictionary was pawned by William Benson of North Street on 11 June 1778 with other items and was unclaimed.

People tried to keep up appearances for as long as possible, but eventually some would be forced to succumb to the pressures of life at the time. Joseph Greenup of Feasegate could have put on a fine show of china and table items at meal times – at least, he could have done until 19 September 1777, for on that date he pledged 'half a dozen cups and saucers, a cream boat and sugar basin, all china, one bowl, two wine glasses, one canister, one decanter and one cruet' for only 4s-0d. Joseph never called back for his tableware, so the pawnbroker had struck a good deal on them.

Robert Rudd led a curious life. Frequently on his travels round York, he would have been seen carrying a tin fender to the pawnbroker's (firstly on 21 November 1777, then recorded throughout the pledge book). It is a mystery why he would carry it from his home in Far Water Lane to Lady Peckett's Yard in the morning, only to redeem it later the same day after paying interest, and then to bring it back the next morning. He was also spotted on many days with a pair of tongs or a fire poker, or even both, under his arm. Between 14 October 1777 and Christmas the following year, he was a frequent visitor to the pawn shop but with a complete gap of three months in the summer time. More than 85% of Robert Rudd's pledges were for 2s-0d or less and he rarely left any item pledged for more than a few days, as the following table shows.

Redeemed after	Number of Pledges
0 days (i.e. same day)	14
1 day	44
2 days	25
3 days	17
4 days	8
5 days	20
6 to 14 days	16
More than 14 days	26
Unredeemed	6
Total	**176**

Three of Robert Rudd's pledges are marked in the pledge book as 'Redeemed' but no redemption date is given, even though the shop was not particularly busy at that time – from the other entries, it is probable that they were redeemed after either one or two days, and are included in the table above like that.

And what did Robert Rudd pawn? Usually household items, as shown below.

Robert Rudd's Pledges	Number of Times Pledged
Tin fender	31
Seeing or looking glass	27
Pair of tongs	21
Apron	12
Bonnet or hat	12
Cloak	11
Poker	11
Stockings	11
Fire shovel	9
Coat	8
Waistcoat	8
Handkerchief	7
Gown	6
Petticoat	6
Pair of shoes/pumps	5
Pillow	5
Bedside carpet	3
Book or Bible	3
Candlestick	3

Valuables

Many people pawned their valuables, often complete with engraved family initial, suggesting they had fallen on hard times compared with their parents and ancestors. Some subsequently found sufficient money to redeem the family heirlooms, others did not. Hannah Rice of Coppergate on 26 October 1778 said goodbye to one salt, one tablespoon, two teaspoons and one pair of sugar nippers, all silver and marked with R W H, for 18s-0d; on 17 October 1778 Mary Sorry of Newgate asked Charles Pearson to pledge one silver gill and two silver salts each marked S T M and received £1-1s-0d; on 15 August 1777 George Ireland pawned fifteen silver coat buttons, each marked G I, for 1s-0d each. The latter two pledges were redeemed within one month.

Some people actually pawned their money. John Phillips pawned two crown pieces for 6s-0d (a crown was worth 5s-0d)[20] and Mrs Dent of Petergate pawned five crown pieces along with two silver watches, two silver tablespoons, twelve silver teaspoons, one silver cup and four yards of lace, all for eight guineas (£8-8s-0d).[21] On 23 May 1778 Joseph Hick of Foss Bridge brought in one doubtful (in the pawnbroker's opinion) gold coin dated 1750 and some old silver coins, which he reclaimed six months later. The pawnbroker's would be a place of safe keeping to the customers, where they could leave their valuables and confidently expect them to be still there when they were next wanted.

From 16 to 23 August 1777 and from 22 to 29 August 1778, the annual horse racing meeting was held on the Knavesmire in York, followed by the customary grand ball at the Assembly Rooms in Blake Street. These events were an important part of the social scene of the day and the well-to-do would move into their town houses in York for the season. People came into the city from a wide area and several of them called at the pawn shop in Lady Peckett's Yard looking for funds. They came from Pocklington, Newton-on-Derwent, Great Driffield, North Dalton on the Wolds, Leeds, Doncaster, Pontefract, Newcastle-under-Lyme and Sutton-in-Ashfield near Mansfield in 1777, and from Stillingfleet, Knaresborough, Sowerby near Thirsk, Doncaster and Sheffield in 1778.

Daniel Eyre or Hare from Doncaster pawned (and redeemed) his silver watch in both race weeks, but not the same watch. George Parrott, staying at Francis Tayler's in Swinegate, was not so lucky. He pawned his silver watch for £1-11s-6d during the 1777 race week but he must have been unsuccessful in his selection of horses to wager on for he never reclaimed it – it was sold on 27 May 1780 for an unspecified amount.

A silver watch was a predictable way to raise cash quickly. Most of the watches pawned were listed with the name of the manufacturer and serial number, making it obvious when an individual watch was pawned more than once. John Nottage travelled the ten miles from Tadcaster on 22 July 1778 to pawn his 'new silver watch' for two guineas (£2-2s-0d). He returned just within the forfeit time of three months and re-pawned it, again for two guineas, along with a pair of sheets for 7s-0d – a rather strange combination, or had his wife sent him into York with their most valuable possessions? He was again given a forfeit time of three months for his watch, but the pledge book does not show it as redeemed. However, the three months would have expired in

January 1779, which was after the end of the book, so he may have reclaimed his watch and sheets without the pledge book being updated.

The trail of the silver watch number 169 made by R Motley of London is very interesting. On 18 July 1777, it was pawned for 15s-0d by Pendock Vame, an apprentice with Mr Firth of Coney Street, who redeemed it on 4 November even though he had lost his duplicate ticket. On 17 November, the watch was back, but this time the owner was John Turner of North Street. He redeemed it three days later and must have sold it at once, for the very next day Sarah Kennedy of Swinegate brought it in, redeeming it seven days later. One wonders what explanations were given to the pawnbroker, since it was an offence to pawn another person's goods without declaring them as such for recording in the pledge book.

The landed gentry had a choice of what to pledge; not for them the poverty which necessitated a pledge of a mere two buttons. In the spring of 1778, Squire Mason rode the fourteen or so miles from Allerton Mauleverer (near Knaresborough) to visit the pawnbroker in York. In March 1778, he pawned his silver watch for 17s-0d. Five months later, he redeemed it but left six silver teaspoons in its place, each engraved with the initials H M, for which he received 12s-0d. He gives the impression that he valued his silver teaspoons more than his watch, for four weeks later, during the race week, he redeemed the family teaspoons and re-pledged his original watch, this time for 14s-0d. Like George Parrott, he seems to have lost his money at the races and his watch to the pawnbroker, for he was not recorded as redeeming it, but he *was* able to bequeath the family silver to future generations.

Alexander Lenox Esquire of Saint Saviourgate visited the pawn shop only twice: once on 19 January 1778 to pledge his gold watch and his stone ring, each for £6-6s-2d, a curious sum, and again the following day to redeem them both. He would have been the type of customer the pawnbroker would have dreamed about – a customer who accepted a large cash sum which would generate good interest charges, who redeemed the pledge quickly, who pawned saleable items in case they were unclaimed and whose items took up hardly any space in storage.

Family and Friends

Some people asked members of their family to visit the pawnbroker for them, some asked their servants and some asked friends and acquaintances. In total, 114 pledges were recorded as being made on behalf of someone else, a very small number when compared to the total number of pledges recorded – almost eleven thousand in all.

The following table shows who most frequently asked another person to pawn their goods.

Brought for	Number of Times
Baythorn(e)	7
Bradley	2
Bradshaw	2
Car(e)y	2
Fairb(o)urn(e)	13
Hair/Hare	4
Hart	3
Plowman	2
Sledmire	2
Smith	3
Tate	5
Wheelhouse	2
Wil(l)son	2
Wood	5
Young	2

And the table below shows who most frequently brought in those goods.

Brought by	Number of Times
Aspinall	2
Beeforth	10
Bowman	7
Clarkson	2
Crampton	5
Gardiner	5
Girdler	2
Gordon	2
Hair/Hare	4
Heslop(e)	2
Metcalfe	3
Milner	2
Moor(e)	4
Smith	2

Other People's Property

One might assume that all the items pawned did, in fact, belong to the stated owners, but this was not always the case, especially if the owners lived near Fossgate! Remember, the part of Lady Peckett's Yard leading to Fossgate was once called Cheat's Lane and apparently with good reason. Jane Newcombe of Fossgate received 5s-0d for a great coat on 4 March 1778, but the next day the coat's owner arrived in the shop to reclaim it, stating that she had stolen it from him. Barbara Topham of Fossgate was noted in the register as having pledged a stolen silk hat.[22]

Ann Moyser moved from Walmgate to Fossgate in May 1778 and quickly picked up the bad habits of some of the neighbours. On 9 June 1778, she pawned a checked apron which was not hers for 1s-0d. Four months later her dishonest deed was exposed, for the comment in the pledge book reads 'this apron was challenged by Castlegate overseers [as] belonging to Sarah Wood & they had it out but without ye duplicate'. It appears that Sarah Wood did not miss her checked apron for many weeks, although it may have taken four months for her to track it down and to convince the overseers of the parish that they ought to help her.

This was not the first time that the paths of Sarah Wood and the Castlegate overseers had crossed. Sarah Wood herself pledged items on only two days, 23 and 24 January 1778. Her four pledges (two yards of check, 2½ yards of cloth, a pair of stays, a checked apron and a handkerchief) were all redeemed by someone else: three by Mr Wright, Tea man, including the checked apron on 30 April, and the fourth by the Castlegate overseers themselves. There appears to have been more to Sarah Wood's life than we know about.

The following notice in the *York Chronicle* of the time details many items pawned by Thomas Grimshaw of Dringhouses 'which are supposed to have been stolen'.

> STOLEN GOODS.
>
> Whereas the following Articles were
>
> found in the house of THOMAS GRIMSHAW,
>
> at Dringhouses, (now confined in the House of Correction in York) viz. Half a piece of 16d black ribbon – Half a piece of 14d pink ditto, edg'd with white – One silk handkerchief – 2 ³⁄₈ yards of yard-wide book muslin – 2 ³⁄₈ yards of Scotch gauze – 7 remnants of white lace – 31 remnants of coloured ribbons – One linen handkerchief – Four small remnants of lawn – and three small ditto Irish cloth.
>
> Also were found, Pawnbroker's Tickets for the following goods pledged by the said Thomas Grimshaw, viz. A silver watch, pawn'd May 27, 1775 – a silver cream-jug, pawn'd April 12 1776 – Two silver spoons – One plated pint, one gill, knives, forks, table-cloths, and many other things too numerous to mention, all [of] which are supposed to have been stolen.
>
> All persons who have missed any such goods, upon telling the marks, and describing the goods, may see them by applying to Thomas Robson, in Castlegate, York.

York Chronicle & General Advertiser 8 August 1777

Mary Bowman of Peter Lane pawned her husband's shirt without his knowledge, for the note reads 'this shirt belonged to her man and was obliged to let him have it and never got anything for it'.[23] One could imagine Mr Bowman as a large, fierce man as he demanded his property back, or perhaps he was merely extremely persistent.

Ann Crampton of Jubbergate and Mary Metcalfe of Walmgate brought in a tea kettle each, which were subsequently redeemed by their respective landladies who said the tea kettles belonged to them.[24] This was not the only time Mary Metcalfe pawned goods belonging to her landlady – on 22 November 1777, she pawned a box iron and heater which her landlady retrieved on 16 May the following year.

It was illegal to pawn someone else's property without declaring it to be so, but Mary Metcalfe seemed none too fussy about this. Besides the two pledges belonging to her landlady, the following items which she pledged *may* have belonged to other people for they were redeemed, not by Mary, but by the people noted below.

Mary's Item	May Have Belonged To
1 pair of tongs, 1 poker and 1 fire shovel	Jane Rudd (a relative of Robert Rudd perhaps)
1 old brass pan	Jane Masser's brother
2 pairs of kid gloves	Jane Ruclus
1 black silk cloak	Ann Kitson

Conditions for Pledges

It might be said that George Fettes, the pawnbroker of Lady Peckett's Yard, could be a kind-hearted man, sympathetic to the pleadings of his customers when he chose. On almost 700 occasions, he stipulated that items were to be forfeited if not redeemed within a set period, which varied from 'next Saturday night' to 'twelve months', the most frequent being one month, but he appears to have regularly over-looked his own conditions.

Nevertheless, he could decide that enough is enough. On 14 July 1777, Hannah Priestley of Aldwark accepted 11s-2d on three pledge tickets, listing '4½ yards of new cloth, one new checked handkerchief, three pieces of new cloth, one checked apron, one cap and a pair of sleeves'. On 2 August 1777, she pawned items on a further five pledge tickets totalling 12s-1d (one washing gown, one new tea kettle, one flannel petticoat, two yards of check, four yards of flannel), but when she offered him a sixth item, namely her 'Silk Petticoat Quilted', she received 3s-6d and a warning – 'Agreed this day on account of so much being advanced on this ticket that she is not to be allowed to demand the 3 tickets of the 14th of July 1777 whilst this ticket is redeemed'. This meant that the quilted silk petticoat had to be redeemed before the items pledged on 14 July were redeemed. She never redeemed the petticoat, but did redeem one of the tickets from 14 July, but not until 10 June the following year, by which time the pawnbroker would surely have forgotten the conditions which he himself had imposed.

The pawnbroker even gave her a further £1-6s-6d only three days after the warning, this time against seven pledge tickets (one shift, one pair of sheets, three yards of Russia cloth, one Barcelonia red silk handkerchief, one shift, one cotton handker-chief, three yards of towelling, ¾ yards of lawn, ½ a yard of muslin, one petticoat, one pair of covered stays, one muslin apron and one linen handkerchief). Five of the seven tickets were redeemed, but none within the forfeit time. Her final pledge was on 17 August 1778 (a pair of old stays and an old bonnet for 2s-0d) which she redeemed less than two weeks later and was not seen in the shop again. Was the pawnbroker glad to see the back of her, or did he regret losing one of his regulars? Probably the former, since he was left with more than 40% of her pledges taking up space in his warehouse, for which no interest was receivable.

It was not unknown for the pawnbroker to advance money without any goods being pawned in return. For example, Mrs Moore of Girdlergate on 17 October 1777 appears to have redeemed her 1s-0d pledge ('on this ticket only') on the same day, probably plus interest, and Mrs Brooks of Hungate on 19 August 1777 received 6d 'lent on the ticket only' which she redeemed nine days later.

Occasionally, a customer was allowed to redeem goods without any charge for interest but this was extremely infrequent. James Rodwell of Skeldergate managed to take home his shift, one pair of thread stockings, three child's jams, one silver spoon engraved with S R, a pincushion, a sheet and two bibles only five days after pledging them in September 1778 for 14s-0d, but without handing over anything by way of interest. The pawnbroker may have felt compassionate towards James, but he would also have been aware that, in his warehouse, were a few more of James' family's possessions – namely a black crape gown, 1¼ yards of flowered linen and three silver teaspoons – which had been pledged for £1-5s-0d on the same day as the other items. The expected interest on this sum would have helped to soften any disappointment felt by the pawnbroker.

Some of the Items Pledged

As mentioned previously, people from far and wide used the pledge shop in Lady Peckett's Yard and they pledged an extensive assortment of items. Some customers struggled in with a bed or an oak tea-table or a china tea service, others brought more portable items like a gold ring or a silver spoon, or a few buttons. All of them were in need, and, without the state help with which most of us in the twenty-first century have grown up, they were forced to raise money by any means they could.

Among the more interesting items they brought for pledge were:

Item	Brought By
• 2 bunches of willows	Ann Sledmire of Little Shambles on 9 Aug 1777, 6s-0d, redeemed 13 Nov 1777
• a box containing some artificial flowers	Isabella Brown of Walmgate Bar on 16 Aug 1777, 1s-6d, unclaimed
• 6 pairs of hollows and rounds	John Tate of Goodramgate on 26 Aug 1777, 4s-0d, redeemed 30 Jun 1778
• 1 quart bottle of oil of peppermint	Mrs Dale of Walmgate on 12 Sep 1777, £1-1s-0d, redeemed 21 Jan 1778
• 1 old fashioned looking glass	Jane Newcomb of Fossgate on 6 Oct 1777, 1s-6d, redeemed 24 Oct 1777

Item	Brought By
• 1 gun	Francis Benson of Walmgate on 1 Nov 1777, 6s-6d, unclaimed
• 1 small picture of a nun	Isabella Brown of Walmgate Bar on 19 Nov 1777, 6d, unclaimed
• a bird net	Sarah Hill of Little Shambles on 21 Nov 1777, 3s-6d, unclaimed
• 1 hand saw	William Oliver of Walmgate on 22 Nov 1777, 3s-0d, redeemed 28 Feb 1778
• 1 old saddle	Thomas Ruclus of Walmgate on 24 Nov 1777, 3s-0d, unclaimed
• leather for a pair of shoes	Mrs Moore of Girdlergate on 11 Feb 1778, 1s-9d, redeemed 13 Feb 1778
• 1 clothes brush	Robert Dixon of Ouse Bridge on 26 Feb 1778, 6d, unclaimed
• 1 oak corner cupboard	Ester Benson of Walmgate on 2 May 1778, 4s-0d, unclaimed
• some odd things	Ann Bird of Skeldergate on 23 May 1778, 1s-0d, redeemed two days later
• some goose and hen feathers in a mat basket	Jane Modisty of Saint Saviourgate on 26 Jun 1778, 1s-8d, unclaimed
• 1 old fire poker & shovel almost broke through	George Metcalfe of Far Water Lane on 27 Aug 1778, 6d, redeemed 6 Oct 1778
• 1 sword	Mr John Shawn of Coney Street on 29 Aug 1778, 6s-0d, redeemed 12 Sep 1778
• 1 pair of garden sheers	John Johnson of Fishergate on 17 Oct 1778, 1s-0d, redeemed 27 Oct 1778
• 1 German flute	Edward Addison of North Street on 31 Oct 1778, 2s-6d, redeemed 15 Dec 1778

Item	Brought By
• 1 pair of black everlasting breeches	Thomas Callis out of Micklegate Bar on 13 Nov 1778, 3s-6d, redeemed 8 Dec 1778
• 1 child's gown and a pair of stockings 1 of them with the needles in it	Eliz Firth of North Street on 7 Dec 1778, 1s-1d, unclaimed

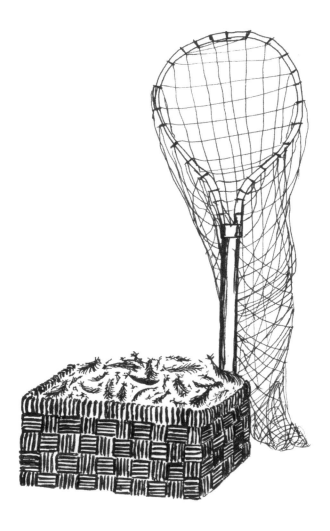

4

The Finances of the Business

In order to be a pawnbroker, a large sum of money was required to start the business – the National Pawnbrokers Association estimates that about £50,000 to £100,000 would be necessary today, which converts to almost £500 to £1,000 in the 1770s. The start-up requirements would be similar in both periods – premises for the customers to call at, shop fittings to provide a little privacy for customers, security features both inside the building and out, a pledge book, pledge tickets, storage facilities which must be capable of expansion if the business prospered, staff, advertising and so on.

Pledges Deposited

Saturday was the busiest day of the week for receiving pledges at the office in Lady Peckett's Yard – 24% of the goods came in during that day, with Monday a close second at 21%. Just over half the goods came in on the remaining four days, each day being very like the other three but usually showing a slight decline each day as the week progressed. The money paid out to customers on each day naturally reflected the same pattern (Saturday 26%, Monday 21%). Remember, each pledge which the pawnbroker took in resulted in him handing over some cash.

The next table shows how many pledges were left at the York shop on each day of the week during the whole eighteen months covered by the pledge book.

Day of the Week Pledged	Pledges Deposited during July 1777 to December 1778	
	Number	Value
Monday	2,343	£434-15s-2d
Tuesday	1,591	£287-2s-5d
Wednesday	1,554	£267-3s-11d
Thursday	1,432	£275-9s-11d
Friday	1,382	£242-11s-8d
Saturday	2,615	£531-16s-9d
Sunday	No pledges	
Totals	**10,917**	**£2,038-19s-10d**

The average value advanced against a pledge during the period recorded in the pledge book was 3s-9d, but this figure masks the great variety of sums advanced. The greatest sum for a single pledge was given to Mrs Fountaine of Ousegate who received ten guineas (£10-10s-0d) for a diamond buckle.[25] This was the only time she pawned anything (as recorded in the book), but the pawnbroker's confidence in her was rewarded for she returned four months later to redeem it. Only 296 pledges (2.7%) were for £1 or more, as shown below.

Number of Pledges	Value Received per Pledge
8,718	less than 5s-0d
1,346	5s-0d to 9s-11d
557	10s-0d to 19s-11d
229	£1-0s-0d to £1-19s-11d
23	£2-0s-0d to £2-19s-11d
13	£3-0s-0d to £3-19s-11d
13	£4-0s-0d to £4-19s-11d
6	£5-0s-0d to £5-19s-11d
5	£6-0s-0d to £6-19s-11d
4	£7-0s-0d to £7-19s-11d
2	£8-0s-0d to £8-19s-11d
0	£9-0s-0d to £9-19s-11d
1	£10 or over

Hidden within these two summaries are Mrs Iveson of Bilton and John Iveson Esquire of Holgate. It seems likely that these two people were related, for their pledges were recorded on three consecutively numbered tickets, and they were in all probability mother and son. What a sad tale they would have told – creditors had gathered to recover debts from the family of George Iveson, recently of Bilton but now deceased, and money had to be found to pay them.[26] So the family raised as much money as they could in the quickest manner they could think of, but surely not without heartache. Between them, on 5 November 1778, they pawned one silver coffee pot, one silver tea pot, one cream pot, one small waiter, six silver tablespoons, one silver tumbler, one pair of silver nippers, one gold watch, one large and two small silver waiters and one large soup spoon. The total sum received was a generous £23-8s-0d and was greater than a pawnbroker was permitted to advance on a single pledge, hence the three tickets. Not one of their items was redeemed, which was hardly surprising in the circumstances, so the pawnbroker would have had to forgo all the interest which would have accrued, as well as having to sell the items at a good price to recover his costs. On the same day, other goods were pledged for a further £1-4s-1d but only £4-16s-3d was received from customers who redeemed items (plus an unspecified sum for interest) – a net cash outflow of almost £20 and not a good day's business for him! But he would have had the satisfaction of knowing that he had significantly helped a family as well as their creditors. Unfortunately, the money proved insufficient to rescue the Iveson family from their dire predicament, as four months later John Iveson was also bankrupt and was forced to sell his elegant household furniture.[27]

Mrs Fountaine had pledged her diamond buckle on a Thursday and John and Mrs Iveson had also pledged their silverware on a Thursday. These four pledge tickets alone amounted to £33-18s-0d, which explains why the total value of the items pledged on Thursdays appears to be out of step with the total number of items pledged on those days. The pawnbroker would have kept a substantial sum of cash on the premises to cater for such occasions, notably during the race week each August.

The smallest loan of only 2d was given on six occasions, specifically to Ann Crampton of Jubbergate for one tin tinder box (just two days before her landlady's tea kettle came to her notice),[28] to John Nailer of North Street for two bibs and one pair of child skirts,[29] to Mary Wilson of Water Lane and Bishophill for firstly one child skirt, secondly one cap, thirdly for one small handkerchief,[30] and to Mrs Smith of Colliergate for one pair of stockings.[31] The most common amount loaned was one shilling, given in exchange for 1,542 pledges (14% of the total number of pledges).

Sometimes a customer had several articles for pawn but wanted them to be recorded on separate pledge tickets. This would enable the debt to be paid off gradually when the money was available and the articles could be taken home as soon as possible. On 20 January 1778, Eliz Wilson of Middle Water Lane pawned, on seven tickets, a white gown; a washing gown; a white petticoat and tablecloth; a black quilted petticoat and a green calamanco petticoat; a garnet ring with two stones missing; a pair of silver buckles; and a pair of white silk stockings, for a total of £2-9s-0d. This proved insufficient for her needs, for she was back ten days later with a blue crepe gown, a further washing gown and two laced handkerchiefs on three tickets for 18s-0d. Of these items, she only redeemed the first washing gown and the pair of silver buckles, both after twenty-one days. Surely the three gowns and the three petticoats which she abandoned would have been more use to her than the silver buckles, but they were not what she valued most.

Pledges Redeemed

Just as Saturdays and Mondays were the busiest days for pledges being deposited, they were also the busiest days for pledges being redeemed. However, Saturdays far exceeded Mondays in this case, in both number of customers and money changing hands. 41% of all the pledges redeemed were collected on a Saturday, for 37% of the money. Mondays accounted for 14% of all the pledges redeemed and 16% of the money. The busiest single day was Saturday 28 March 1778, when 46 customers pledged goods and received £10-9s-7d, and 78 customers redeemed pledges for £12-11s-3d. It must have been pandemonium!

The next table shows on which days the pledges were redeemed from the York shop during the whole eighteen months covered by the pledge book.

Day of the Week Redeemed	Pledges Redeemed of those Deposited During July 1777 to December 1778	
	Number	Value
Monday	1,122	£233-9s-8d
Tuesday	977	£217-1s-6d
Wednesday	859	£157-5s-7d
Thursday	904	£160-17s-6d
Friday	947	£153-14s-2d
Saturday	3,362	£551-17s-9d
Sunday	42	£8-12s-1d
Totals	**8,213**	**£1,482-18s-3d**

Some pledges were surprisingly redeemed on the day they were pawned, others remained at the pawnbroker's for much longer. The most common duration was a mere five days: 601 pledges were redeemed after five days and 192 pledges were redeemed on the day they were deposited. People often redeemed their goods after a multiple of seven days, well-illustrated by 44 pledges redeemed after 27 days and 51 pledges after 29 days, but between these were the 100 pledges redeemed after 28 days.

The item remaining the longest time in the shop appears to be the silver watch belonging to John Smith of Stonegate. He pawned it on 30 October 1777 and it was either redeemed or sold on 24 June 1780. This was an unusually long time – the vast majority of redemptions were made within the year and more than 25% were redeemed within a week.

By no means were all pledges redeemed. Almost 25% of the recorded pledges were abandoned in the pawnbroker's warehouse and the table on the following page illustrates this well.

Month	Pledges Deposited		Pledges Redeemed	
	Number (Goods to Store)	**£ Value (Money to Customer)**	**Number (Goods Removed)**	**£ Value (Money to Pawnbroker)**
July 1777	394	£50-13s-6d	79	£13-3s-0d
August 1777	585	£141-10s-3d	307	£55-13s-8d
September 1777	673	£110-0s-7d	309	£47-5s-5d
October 1777	742	£139-11s-1d	429	£70-11s-3d
November 1777	644	£127-15s-7d	483	£73-14s-1d
December 1777	712	£131-13s-1d	487	£102-5s-3d
January 1778	859	£159-5s-10d	532	£102-13s-10d
February 1778	761	£138-1s-0d	500	£102-3s-10d
March 1778	719	£133-8s-7d	641	£112-14s-10d
April 1778	562	£96-5s-9d	547	£99-14s-7d
May 1778	630	£119-2s-4d	703	£139-13s-6d
June 1778	547	£89-1s-11d	538	£93-6s-8d
July 1778	451	£84-19s-1d	424	£84-8s-5d
August 1778	510	£123-0s-5d	548	£105-14s-5d
September 1778	485	£91-6s-3d	355	£57-10s-10d
October 1778	587	£113-5s-7d	463	£71-8s-0d
November 1778	523	£106-17s-6d	411	£75-1s-1d
December 1778	533	£83-1s-6d	449	£71-1s-4d
March 1779			3	10s-1d
April 1779	There is no record of the		2	3s-8d
May 1779	pledges during these months		1	14s-0d
December 1779			1	£1-15s-0d
May 1780			1	£1-11s-6d
Totals	**10,917**	**£2,038-19s-10d**	**8,213**	**£1,482-18s-3d**

Some of the early pages in the pledge book are damaged with pieces missing, inevitably resulting in the totals for the early months being understated. The final pledge recorded was for 26 December 1778, so that month is incomplete also. The two columns in the table above dealing with redeemed pledges refer to the number and value of pledges redeemed in the month stated – they were pledged during the same month or any previous month. The table does not show how many of a month's pledges were redeemed in the month they were pledged.

In total, 2,704 pledges were not redeemed, at a nominal cost to the pawnbroker of £556-1s-7d.

Inevitably, some days saw more customers redeeming their goods than other days. On seventy-one days, five or fewer pledges were redeemed, yet on twenty-eight days, there were more than fifty pledges redeemed each day. The most usual number of redemptions was between six and fifteen per day.

The customer who left the most articles unredeemed was Mrs Fountaine of Fossgate. During the period of the pledge book, she redeemed seventy-three pledge tickets but abandoned thirty others to the pawnbroker, forsaking the following items: a gold ring, a silky gown, a black silk hat, two flat irons, a pair of cloth breeches, three waistcoats, a black silk bonnet, a scarlet cloak, a cotton gown, two other gowns, a pillow, a shirt, four checked aprons, one flowered apron, three child frocks, a cap, three yards of edging lace, a snuff box, fifteen yards of linen cloth in two pieces, 7½ yards of black lace, two handkerchiefs, a boys waistcoat, two odd plated spurs, another frock, two pairs of child skirts and a pair of stockings. Apart from the gold ring (which may have been her wedding ring), the snuff box, the spurs and the lace, everything else might be classed as a necessity. Assuming she was an honest person, and there is no indication to suppose otherwise, how could she continue to survive in a reasonable manner without all these items? And how would she manage when she next needed money?

As the days went by, the pawnbroker would have needed more and more cash-on-hand since there were more pledges deposited than there were redeemed, so more money was paid out to customers than was taken from them. Charges for interest and storage would have reduced the deficit a little, but the unwanted pledges which had accumulated in the warehouse had to be removed. Frequent sales of goods were essential, both to increase his ready money and to make room for future pledges.

Below is a newspaper advertisement for a sale, fourteen years after the pledge book was discontinued. It shows that George Fettes was a licensed auctioneer in addition to being a pawnbroker and he was still prospering despite the aforementioned difficulties.

UNREDEEMED PLEDGES
To be SOLD by PUBLIC AUCTION,
On Wednesday the 17th day of April next, at ten o'clock in the forenoon, at the house of Mr. GEORGE FETTES, licensed auctioneer, in Lady Peckett's Yard, Pavement, York.
Several LOTS of UNREDEEMED
PLEDGES, consisting of PLATE, WATCHES, WEAR-
ING APPAREL, &c. – Those who are interested in this
notice, may apply before the day of sale, and either pay off
the interest or redeem their goods.
GEORGE FETTES, Auctioneer.

York Herald 9 March 1793

It was not possible to make a precise analysis of how many pledges were redeemed on a particular date, since the redemption date was written against the entry dated when the goods were pledged. For example, goods pledged during June 1777, before the book begins, could have been redeemed in June, or during the time-span of the book, or after the book finishes. Items redeemed during the time-span of the book could be counted, but there is no way of knowing how those daily figures should be augmented for goods pledged before the book begins.

In addition, the pawnbroker employed at least one assistant who was not always sure what day it was. Joseph Smith, the quack doctor, pawned his watch on 11 September 1778 and redeemed it on 26 September, yet he was recorded apparently re-pawning it two days earlier on 24 September. Of the goods pawned on 15 and 16 April 1778, nine pledges were apparently redeemed on 14 April! If the entries refer to 14 April 1779, they would be the only days showing so many redemptions exactly one year later. It is far more likely that the assistant was less than fully alert and, as the customers had taken their goods away with them, he may not have thought accuracy to be very important.

These are not the only obvious mistakes. Forty-two pledges were recorded as being redeemed on a Sunday. Presumably this is an error on the part of the pawnbroker or his assistant, since goods were never pawned on a Sunday, but this, too, would affect an analysis of redemption dates.

As mentioned in Chapter 2, there are forty-four damaged pages in the pledge book, which has resulted in about 200 pledges having their redemption date physically missing. In the database and its analysis, these entries had to be treated as 'not redeemed', since there was no evidence to the contrary. They all occurred during July to September 1777 and will undoubtedly have resulted in the total number of redemptions being understated, although by less than 2%. All these factors have added to the difficulty in assessing exactly how busy the shop was on any particular day.

General Trading

The pledge book itself occasionally shows what life was like in the pawnbroking trade in the eighteenth century. After totalling the value of the pledges on 1 December 1777 is the entry '3 lb of candles 1s-7d'. Exactly one week later, '1 quire of ticket paper' was bought for 1s-6d and the following day, a further 3 lb of candles for 1s-7d. Unfortunately these were the only purchases noted regarding day-to-day running costs, what today might be termed 'petty cash' purchases, and there is no indication of how long such supplies might have lasted.

Business at this pawnbroker's slackened off during the second half of 1778, as the following table shows.

Period	Total Number of Pledges	Total Value of Pledges
July to December 1777	3,750	£701-4s-1d
January to June 1778	4,078	£735-5s-5d
July to December 1778	3,089	£602-10s-4d

As with all statistics, the sample must be of sufficient size to give accurate results and to show reliable trends. It could be that the figures for the second half of 1777 were unusually high rather than those for 1778 being unusually low, despite the fact that the information for the first period is incomplete due to the damaged pages. What cannot be disputed is that the shop was visited by 18% fewer customers throughout the second half of 1778. During the York race week in August, twenty-three watches were pawned during 1777 but only nine during 1778. Life may have become a little easier for the citizens of York, or they might have found other ways of making ends meet. Perhaps this pawnbroker had competition in the form of another pawn-broking business opening in the vicinity, even perhaps charging a lower rate of interest to encourage new clients, although there is no corroboration of this in the surviving directories of York for the period.

Nevertheless, the underlying pattern of each week's business remained unaltered, with Saturday and Monday seeing the rush of people eager to have some money in their pockets.

5

The Pawnbroker and the Law

1757 – 1800

The pawnbroking business in Lady Peckett's Yard was regulated by the statute of 1757 (30 Geo2 C24) which was 'An act for the more effectual punishment of persons who shall attain, or attempt to attain, possession of goods or money, by false or untrue pretences; for preventing the unlawful pawning of goods; for the easy redemption of goods pawned'. The act was not specific to the pawnbroking trade, for it was also 'For preventing gaming in public houses by journeymen, labourers, servants and apprentices'.

This act obliged the pawnbroker to keep a register of the items he accepted for pawn, listing for each pledge:

- the description of the goods or chattels
- the sum of money advanced
- the date of the transaction
- the name and address of the person offering the goods
- the name and address of the goods' owner if a person did not bring in their own property

The penalty for non-compliance with the act was £5 for each occurrence.

A duplicate copy of the pledge ticket (essentially a receipt) showing the above details could be obtained by the customer, if he so chose, but he had to pay for the privilege: ½d if the goods were pawned for less than £1, 1d if they were pawned for up to £5 and 2d thereafter. As the main purpose of pawning an item was to raise money, it is a reasonable assumption that the majority of customers would not have bothered to ask for a duplicate. However, even those who did obtain one did not always manage to keep it safely. There are about 160 comments in the pledge book noting that the duplicate ticket did not come in – the reasons given include the ticket was burnt, lost, left at home, thrown into the dirt or stolen.

One of the main reasons behind the 1757 act was to prevent the unlawful pawning of goods, which had become a major problem. A person was to be fined 20s-0d (£1) if he/she pawned goods without leave of the owner and, on non-payment, was to be committed to jail for fourteen days with hard labour, but would be released sooner if the fine was paid. As a further incentive to get the fine paid somehow, the prisoner was to be publicly whipped after eleven of those days if he/she was still in jail. The 20s-0d was to be used towards compensating injured parties and defraying the costs of prosecution; anything left over was to be paid to the overseers of the parish in which the offence was committed, for the use of the poor of that parish.

If the pawnbroker knowingly (difficult to prove) took in linen or apparel which had been entrusted to someone else to wash, scour, iron, mend or make up, he was fined double the sum given and had to restore the goods to the owner. This is a very paltry penalty when compared with the 20s-0d penalty for pawning someone else's goods. If an owner believed that the pawnbroker was storing an item of his which had been unlawfully pawned, he could apply to a justice for a warrant, which authorised a search of the premises. If the pawnbroker refused access for the search, the peace officer conducting it had authority to force entry but only during daylight hours. A pawnbroker hindering the search was to be fined £5, payable within twenty four hours, and on non-payment he was to be jailed with hard labour for between five days and one month.

The pawnbroker had a duty to take good care of the items while they were in his keeping. If the goods were damaged, or of less value than when pledged (for example, through neglect, wearing, using or even hiring out!), the owner was to be compensated, suggesting that there was extra money to be made on the side before the customers returned for their items. Yet a prudent pawnbroker would have had the foresight to safeguard himself against such a claim. On 8 November 1777, Mrs Addison of York Castle pawned six china cups and saucers and two small china basins for 5s-0d and our pawnbroker wrote in the register 'not answerable to make up loss in case of accident'. It was six months before Mrs Addison reclaimed her china – a severe test of the storage facilities.

The act of 1757 made it easier for customers to recover their property. Previously, even though the borrower had tendered the amount of capital, interest and any other charges made in order to redeem their goods, they frequently had difficulty in getting their hands on the goods and had to commence law suits against the pawnbroker at their own expense. To remedy this, the act stated that goods pawned up to the value of £10 were to be available for recovery for two years and only after that time were they deemed to be forfeited and available for sale. Non-compliance by the pawnbroker would result in him staying in jail until the goods (or suitable compensation) were handed over.

Items originally pawned for £2 or more which were subsequently sold had to be accounted for in another register, listing for each item:

- the date of the sale
- the money received
- the name of the buyer
- the address of the buyer

Any profit, after taking into account interest and storage charges, did not belong to the pawnbroker but was to be paid to the owner on demand. Inspection of an entry in the register of sales cost one penny.

The 1757 act made no mention of the rate of interest which could be levied or the amount of other charges such as for warehouse room – this was not brought in until 1784 – so the pawnbroker was at liberty to charge what he thought the client would or could pay. From the few entries in the pledge book which state the amount of interest paid, it appears that the customers were normally charged about 1d per month or part month per 3s-0d received.

Date Pawned	Pawned By	Value Received	Interest Paid	Period of Interest
19 July 1777	Hannah Priestley	2s-0d	1d	1 month
26 July 1777	...dale	8s-6d	6d	2 months
25 August 1777	Eliz Chip	£2-2s-0d	1s-1d	1 month
26 September 1777	Mally Harrison	12s-0d	4d	1 month
1 December 1777	Mrs Merriott	£2-12s-6d	11s-0d	8 months

Mrs Merriott (see above) of Thursday Market paid 11s-0d in interest charges for her two gowns and her silk cloak after eight months, but never redeemed them.

Later, in 1784, another act was passed (24 Geo3 C42) with the intention to 'explain, amend and render more effectual' the 1757 act. The new act specified the charges which could be made (this included interest and warehouse room): ½d per month or part month for goods not exceeding 2s-6d, and in the same proportion up to 3s-4d per month for goods up to £10. To avoid misunderstandings, the table of rates was to be displayed conspicuously in the shop.

Interest of ½d per month does not sound too expensive, but on further analysis it proves to be very harsh to the customer who desired only a small sum for a short period. A customer accepting 3d and wanting to redeem their goods the next day was to pay 3½d i.e. 16.7% interest, but one receiving 2s-6d and redeeming the next day was still only charged ½d i.e. only 1.7% interest. A pledge for 3d per week for one year, redeemed and repawned each week, resulted in the customer being charged an interest rate of over 850% per annum on the sum borrowed.

Goods pawned for 2s-0d or more were to be described on a duplicate ticket and the customer was obliged to accept the ticket, but he often had to pay for it. For goods valued up to 5s-0d, the ticket was free, but thereafter there was a sliding scale of charges, starting at ½d for items over 5s-0d and up to 10s-0d, to a maximum of 4d per ticket when the sum advanced was over £5. The ticket was to be produced in order to redeem the goods. If less than 2s-0d was advanced, the ticket was not compulsory, so the customer and the pawnbroker had to trust each other.

There were two other major changes: goods need only be kept for one year, not two, and items over 10s-0d may be disposed of only by public auction. Any profit again belonged to the owner of the goods, who still had to pay 1d if he wanted to inspect an entry in the register of sales. The 1784 act also obliged the pawnbroker to have his name and trade displayed in large legible characters over the door of his premises, although it is difficult to understand the reasoning behind this since many people were illiterate and were unlikely to go into the shop by mistake.

A further act passed in the following year (25 Geo3 C48) obliged pawnbrokers to register (the duty was £10 in London and £5 in the country) and another in 1787 (27 Geo3 C37) further regulated the pawnbroker's activities. Hours of trading were restricted: 8am to 9pm in winter and 7am to 10pm in summer. However, there was no restriction at all to Saturday evenings or to the evenings before Good Friday and before Christmas Day. Sunday trading was forbidden. If the money advanced for the goods was less than 5s-0d, the transaction had to be written in the register within four hours and the customer was entitled to receive a duplicate ticket free of charge. Customers were now allowed some period of grace when the interest on the loan was calculated. Unredeemed pledges were forfeited after one year and those for more than 10s-0d could be disposed of only by public auction, which was to be advertised at least twice in a newspaper and a catalogue of the sale was to be published.

The following is just such an advertisement: it is interesting to note that the term 'Pawnbroker' is not used.

PAVEMENT PLEDGE OFFICE

On   Wednesday   the 3rd of   December   next, will be sold by public Auction, by Mr. GEORGE FETTES, Licensed Auctioneer, at his House in Lady Peckett's Yard, Pavement, York, Goods which are forfeited according to Act of Parliament.

The Business carried on as usual by George Fettes, who hopes by unremitting care to merit the Public's Favour.

☞Informations,   respecting lost or   stolen Goods, attended to with the strictest fidelity,   at the above Office.

York Courant 25 November 1788

Yet more acts followed in rapid succession up to 1796 (28 Geo3 C50, 29 Geo3 C57, 31 Geo3 C52, 33 Geo3 C53, 36 Geo3 C87); pawnbrokers clearly had to be men of intelligence to understand and comply with all the fast-changing legislation.

1800 – 1872

The 1800 act (39&40 Geo3 C99) may be regarded as the start of a new era of legislation affecting pawnbrokers. Lord Eldon had considerable influence over it, having made good use of pawnshops in his younger days. Amongst other things, the act stated:

- the rates which could be charged
- farthings (¼d) had to be given in change if the transaction warranted it
- half-months were to be taken into account when calculating the charges
- a customer who was a lodger or housekeeper was to be noted as such when he/she gave his/her abode
- pledges exceeding 5s-0d had to be recorded in the pledge book before the money was given over
- a separate book was to be used to record pledges over 10s-0d
- a lost, destroyed or stolen ticket would be replaced by the pawnbroker for a further charge
- the pawnbroker's profit was to be written on the duplicate ticket when the goods were redeemed and the duplicates had to be retained for a year
- pawned goods were deemed to be forfeit after one year but, if asked to do so, the pawnbroker had to keep goods available for redemption for a further three months
- unredeemed goods pawned for over 10s-0d were to be sold at auction
- all pictures, prints, books, bronzes, statues, busts, carvings in ivory and marble, cameos, intaglios, china, and musical, mathematical and philo-sophical instruments could only be auctioned four times per year on specific days and no other goods were to be for sale on those days

The rate of interest was specified at ½d per month per 2s-6d lent and was to be inclusive of any charge for warehouse room. For the first time half-months were to be taken into account for the benefit of the customer yet, to compensate the pawnbroker a little, half-months did not apply until after the first month had elapsed.

The act worked well, on the whole, for seventy years. It was amended a few times but only slightly. In 1815, the licence duties were increased to £15-0s-0d and £7-10s-0d; in 1840, the reward for reporting illegal rates of interest was abolished; in 1846, the hours of trading were reduced (except for Saturdays and certain other specified dates when the doors could stay open until 11pm); and in 1860, the pawnbroker could charge ½d for the pawn ticket when the loan was for less than 10s-0d – previously, the ticket was free for loans of under 5s-0d so here was more profit for the business.

Pawning an item was usually the quickest way to obtain money legally and the goods would be available to be collected again if personal circumstances improved. At least, that was the theory – some pawnbrokers attempted to evade the law under the pretence that the transaction was a sale and purchase rather than a pledge and redemption. To avoid any possible misunderstandings, the statute passed in 1856 defined precisely who was to be considered a pawnbroker and the penalty for not taking out a licence was set at £50, unless mitigating circumstances could be found on appeal to reduce the fine down to a minimum of £12-10s-0d.

1872 – Present Day

As time went on, the pawnbrokers themselves became dissatisfied with the way their business was being controlled. The Pawnbrokers National Association and the Pawnbrokers Defence Association both worked hard for change, arguing that the 1800 act so interfered with profits that their members could not afford to lend money on bulky articles which required extensive storage facilities. In addition, usury laws had been abolished for everyone except the pawnbroker who advanced less than £10. In 1870, the House of Commons appointed a Select Committee on Pawnbrokers and two years later the result was The Pawnbrokers Act of 1872 (35&36 Vict C93).

This was a major overhaul of the trade – the act repealed the previous acts and restated the terms and conditions of the industry. Every pawnbroker had to be of good character and was required to obtain a yearly license to trade costing £7-10s-0d for each shop kept by him. The act specified the format and wording of the books and documents which must be used. In addition to the date when the pledge was made, the pledge book was to contain nine columns as follows:

- The date of redemption
- The profit charged
- The amount of the loan in £ s d
- The number of the pledge in the month
- The name of the person pawning the goods
- The address of the person pawning the goods
- The name of the goods' owner if other than the pawner
- The address of the goods' owner if other than the pawner
- A list of the articles pawned

The last five columns had to be completed on the day of pawning or within four hours after the end of that day, so that might mean burning the midnight candle after especially busy days.

The 1872 act clearly shows how active the pawnbrokers' lobby groups were when the legislation was being drawn up, for, among other things, the amount of the loan and profit were not subject to a time limit for being recorded. The only significant change to the information to be recorded from that specified in the 1757 act was that the profit charged was to be written in the pledge book. This was supposed to be the true figure, but no doubt an unscrupulous pawnbroker might have noted down less profit than he actually made, and subsequently be liable to pay less tax on his income. The safeguard for this was that a receipt could be obtained by the customer on redemption of the goods, which had to show both the amount of the loan and the profit. The receipt was an optional extra, but, since there was no charge for a receipt, it is likely that the pawnbroker would not be too keen to encourage its uptake, leaving the recording of profit between the pawnbroker and his conscience.

The pawnbroker was permitted to charge ½d for the pawn ticket for loans of 10s-0d and under and 1d for all other tickets. The ticket (but not the charge) was compulsory, thus potentially adding to the charges on the loan before the customer had even left the premises. The rate of interest was increased to ½d per month per 2s-0d lent for pledges up to £2. Pledges for more than £2 were charged ½d per month per 2s-6d lent, an apparently lower rate, but to compensate for this the pawnbroker did not have to take part-months into account.

Pledges for 10s-0d and under which were not redeemed within one year plus one week became the property of the pawnbroker outright – all other pledges remained redeemable until disposed of. Pledges over 10s-0d were to be auctioned and the surplus was to be paid to the customer within three years if he/she asked for it. This sounds fair, but the customer still had to pay 1d to inspect the record of the sale, thus deterring many. The determined customer had not won yet – any deficit on one of his/her pledges could be offset by the pawnbroker against a surplus on another of the same customer's pledges, so the regulations certainly seemed to be favouring the trade.

The pawnbroker was not obliged to hand back goods unless the pledge ticket was produced. Obtaining another copy of a 'lost' ticket would incur further expense for the customer, so it is hoped that the customers found more reliable ways of looking after their tickets than did those who visited George Fettes.

In time, the 1872 act, too, was superseded. Along with the Moneylenders Acts of 1900 to 1927 and the Pawnbrokers Act of 1960, it was repealed and replaced by the Consumer Credit Act of 1974 which was brought into force in stages and was not fully operational until 1985.

While the pawnbroker cannot be recommended in the present day as the first choice for long-term borrowing of large sums of money, he could be very useful for short term loans, even proving cheaper than some other organisations would be. An unauthorised overdraft at a major bank can incur a large fee even if the money is borrowed for only a few days. It could make good economic sense to pawn something in order to pay a utility bill rather than risk disconnection through non-payment and then be obliged to pay a reconnection charge. A pawnbroker will not check your credit rating, nor will he ask why you want the money, so a bet on a horse race will remain confidential just as it did in the eighteenth century.

Pawnbroking has now come right up to date, with unredeemed pledges being advertised for sale on Internet web-sites. At the time of writing, the web-site of one pawnbroker in Northamptonshire advertises cameras, computers, televisions, electrical tools and even golf clubs for sale and offers to accept share certificates and cars as pledges, as well as the usual items of jewellery. Some present day pledges require rather more careful storage than the majority of items which George Fettes encountered more than two hundred years ago.

6

The Owners of the Business

The pawnbroking establishment in Lady Peckett's Yard is believed to have been founded in about 1770, but conclusive objective evidence of the exact date and founder has proved elusive. The earliest objective reference to its existence is in fact the pledge book itself, dating from July 1777. The business would undoubtedly have been helped by the impending closure of George Gibson's pawnbroking enterprise in Shambles, about fifty yards away.

> YORK, May 11, 1773
>
> GEORGE GIBSON, Pawn-Broker, takes
> this Method of acquainting the Public, that he intends
> declining that business, and that he would be obliged to those
> who have any Goods pledged, if they would redeem them as
> soon as possible, as he is going to enter into another Branch of
> Business, and therefore will not take in any more Pawns from
> the Date hereof.

York Courant 11 May 1773

The closure proved more difficult than George Gibson had envisaged. Fourteen months later, he was still advertising that he was determined to give up the pawnbroking business and had opened a shop at the Pavement end of Shambles dealing in 'chimney pieces, glass frames and mouldings for rooms'.[32] By March 1779, he had at last managed to leave pawnbroking behind him, but unfortunately his other business was in difficulties and a notice to his creditors was inserted in the local newspaper. This makes one wonder whether pawnbroking in general was going through a lean time in the mid 1770s, which seems unlikely, or did George Gibson himself find it difficult to make ends meet after competition opened so close to him. He should have persevered – the competition in Lady Peckett's Yard traded for a further two hundred years!

61

George Fettes

George Fettes was born in Edinburgh in about 1754, the son of John Fettes, a merchant,[33] and his wife Grace, and was cousin to Sir William Fettes of Wamphrey,[34] the man who later founded Fettes College in Edinburgh.[35] George spent his early years in Scotland, but then travelled south to York to seek his fortune.

In order to trade within the City boundary at that time, a tradesman had to have been awarded the Freedom of the City of York. There were only three ways in which the Freedom could be granted –

- By patrimony i.e. because a person's father or grandfather was a Freeman
- By apprenticeship
- By paying a fee into the City coffers

Records show that on 30 April 1779 George Fettes was apprenticed to a pawn-broker in York for the usual period of seven years,[36] but there was something very unusual about the arrangement. George was by then twenty-five years old and possibly the oldest apprentice in York, for most apprenticeships began when the young person was in their early teens. The apprenticeship could well have been started as an act of convenience, ensuring that George would be acceptable to the City fathers to run the pawnbroker's shop in his own right when the time came. It is quite probable that George Fettes was perfectly capable of running the business at the time of the pledge book, even before his apprenticeship officially began. It appears that the apprenticeship was not completed satisfactorily, for on 14 April 1794 George had to purchase his Freedom for £25, and by then was aged forty.[37]

The apprenticeship was served under a William Fettes of York, who had only been granted his own Freedom on 30 March 1778 by paying £25. At that time, he said he was a wholesale linen draper.[38] Since part of a pawnbroker's occupation would involve selling pledged garments and cloth which had not been redeemed, he may have thought the term 'linen draper' sounded a little more impressive than 'pawnbroker'. Nothing more is known of this William Fettes, but it is almost a certainty that he and George were related, possibly even brothers.

As already stated, the business was reputed to have been founded in 1770 and by the Fettes family, and there is much evidence to support this – newspaper advertisements declare 'established 1770', as do signs formerly attached to the outside of premises. There is no evidence at all to suggest that it was founded at another time or by another person, despite detailed and thorough research.

In the York Directory of 1781, George Fettes is listed as 'pawn broker, Pavement' – this is not the description of an apprentice. Indeed, a person under training would not even have been listed. An apprentice would have begun learning his trade at a very junior level, probably by sweeping the floor and generally keeping the premises tidy. He would then have progressed to putting away the pawned items into their correct location in the warehouse and retrieving them later. The next promotion would allow him to write out the tickets for the goods (at least two – one ticket to be attached

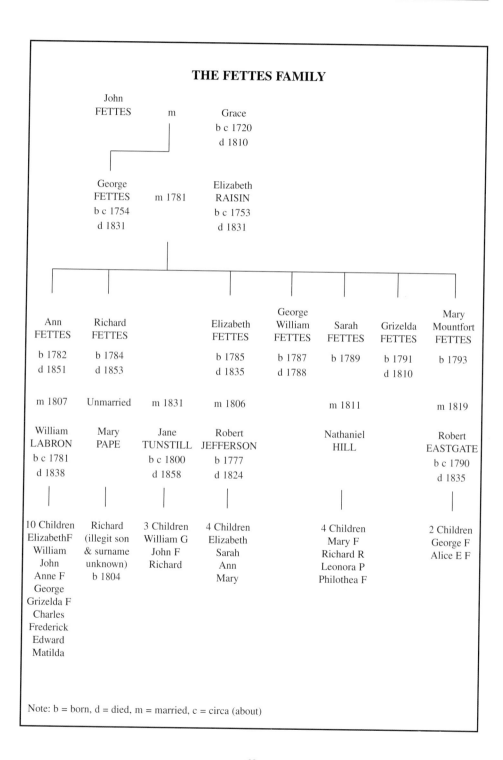

THE FETTES FAMILY

Note: b = born, d = died, m = married, c = circa (about)

to the goods, one kept to be written in the register, and possibly a third if the customer required one), and finally the most responsible task of all – valuing the items brought for pawn and negotiating with the customers.

The pawnbroker's premises in Lady Peckett's Yard remained the residence of George Fettes for close on fifty years until the business was sold in the mid 1820s. He then retired to a house at number 1 Garden Place,[39] just round the corner in the Hungate district, where he died on Sunday 30 January 1831 aged 76, being buried five days later at St Crux Church, Pavement.[40]

His greatest civic honour came in November 1802 when he was elected as one of the two Sheriffs of the City of York,[41] following the unfortunate demise of Sheriff John Hepworth who was taken ill on the day of his inaugural banquet and died from a violent fever two days later. George served the City for more than thirty years – from 1798 he was a commoner for the Walmgate ward until he became Sheriff, and afterwards he was a gentleman of the Twenty-four (who were ex-sheriffs of the city and automatically became members of the City Council on completion of their term of office).[42] During 1816 he became one of the earliest directors of the York Savings Bank, which was founded in that year at the corner of New Street and Davygate, later moving to Saint Helen's Square.[43] He had certainly become a leading and very respectable citizen of York.

On Thursday 3 May 1781 George Fettes married Elizabeth Raisin at her parish church of All Saints North Street in York. George would have known that Thursday was not usually a busy day in his shop and neither was Friday, so he would have been able to enjoy the happy occasion to the full and still be ready for a full day's hectic trading on the Saturday.

His bride was born in February 1753, the child of Richard Raisin, a carpenter and joiner, and she died on Sunday 24 July 1831 aged 78, almost six months after her husband. George and Elizabeth remained married for a few months short of fifty years and were both very highly regarded by their family and friends, as shown by the announcements of their deaths in the local newspaper. They both left wills and the signatures below are from those documents.[44]

On Sunday, the 30th ult., at his house in Garden Place, in his 77th year, Mr. George Fettes, much and deservedly respected by his relatives, friends, and acquaintances.__ He served the office of Sheriff of this city, for a part only of the year 1802, having been elected on the death of Mr. Sheriff Hepworth.

Yorkshire Gazette 5 February 1831

On Sunday, the 24th inst., aged 78, Mrs. Fettes, relict of the late Mr. Sheriff Fettes, of this city. Her long established deep and uniform piety, rendered her truly a mother in Israel__this, connected with her mild and affable disposition, caused her to be esteemed beyond the domestic circle of her relatives; she had many friends who sought her company, and profited by her experienced and judicious counsel. She was a valuable member of the Wesleyan Methodist Society for 56 years, and faithfully discharged the office of a class-leader during the greater part of that time. Her memory will be held in high estimation by her numerous relatives and friends.

Yorkshire Gazette 30 July 1831

Three months after marrying Elizabeth, George received a letter from the great John Wesley asking him to prove that pawnbroking was necessary and lawful in England. His reply must have satisfied the famous man, for when John Wesley visited the city, he often stayed at George's house[45] and he even remarked on George's 'great kindness' at the dinner following the wedding of their mutual friends, John Pawson and Frances Wren, in August 1785.[46]

The Wesleyan Methodists went from strength to strength in York in those days and in the summer of 1830, a 500-seat chapel was opened in Lady Peckett's Yard. How George and Elizabeth must have rejoiced and celebrated! Sadly, that euphoria was not sustained by the congregation, for the chapel was closed in 1858 and offered for sale with the suggestion that it could easily be converted into first-rate business premises.[47]

Life was generally good for George and Elizabeth Fettes – they had seven children born between 1782 and 1793 of whom only one died in infancy – yet when the time came to pass the running of his successful pawnbroker's business to someone else, George Fettes had few options open to him. His elder son, Richard, had been rather a disappointment to his father. Firstly Richard had fathered an illegitimate child when he was aged 20, and secondly Richard's grocery business on Pavement declined almost as soon as he took it over[48] and in 1811 he was declared bankrupt after trading for fewer than five years.[49] George's other son, George William, had died while still an infant. His four surviving daughters had each married businessmen in their own right who were not looking to diversify their operations. His grandsons were all still minors. Consequently, George was forced to sell the business, which he had spent almost fifty years building up, to an outsider. The man to whom he chose to transfer operations was named John Wood.

John Wood

John Wood was born c1795 in Sheffield,[50] the son of Isaac Wood.[51] His older brother, Isaac, was also a pawnbroker so John would probably have developed his skills under his family's guidance.[52] He was in his late twenties or early thirties when George Fettes allowed him to take over of the business in Lady Peckett's Yard, some time between 1823 and 1827. He was certainly the owner on the night of the robbery a week before Christmas 1827.

ROBBERY - On Tuesday morning last, the house of Mr Wood, pawnbroker, situate at Lady Peckett's yard, in this city, was broken into, and a quantity of watches and other articles taken away. The thieves had effected an entrance by the window of the room where pledges are received. Having forced open the shutters, one of them being completely split, they broke through the lead and several panes of glass. On getting into the room, they had used the fire poker in prising the till, which, with a contents, they carried away, also six watches that had been taken in during the day, a number of gold seals, some silver pencil cases, &c. They attempted to force open another drawer, but did not succeed. In a chest was a quantity of linen goods, silk handkerchiefs, &c. but they were not disturbed; nor had the thieves gone into any other room in the house, a fortunate circumstance we understand, as a quantity of valuable plate and other articles, were deposited in some of them. A light being burnt in a chamber, perhaps prevented their further depredations as it could be distinctly seen from the room in which they were. On examining the premises in the morning, it was found that they had attempted to break in at another window in an adjoining room. A noise was heard by a person who lives in the yard betwixt 12 and 1 o'clock, and about 3 o'clock in the morning, the empty till was thrown into the open passage of a public-house in Walmgate – Two persons have been taken into custody on suspicion of being concerned in the above robbery. George Pullen was taken on Wednesday morning, and Joseph Hudson was apprehended by Mr. Pardoe without Micklegate Bar, at six o'clock on Thursday evening. In his hat were found 4 watches, 3 gold seals, a key, and a ring. Hudson said he had found the watches on the road, he being then proceeding towards this city. They were both examined at the Guildhall, on Saturday last, when Hudson again affirmed, that he found the watches out of the Bar, near to a gas lamp, wrapped up in a handkerchief. He was fully committed to the City Jail for trial for the burglary at the next assizes and Pullen was remanded for further examination.

York Courant Monday 24 December 1827

Seven months after the robbery, John Wood celebrated his marriage on 22 July 1828 at his parish church of St Crux to Isabella Thornham.

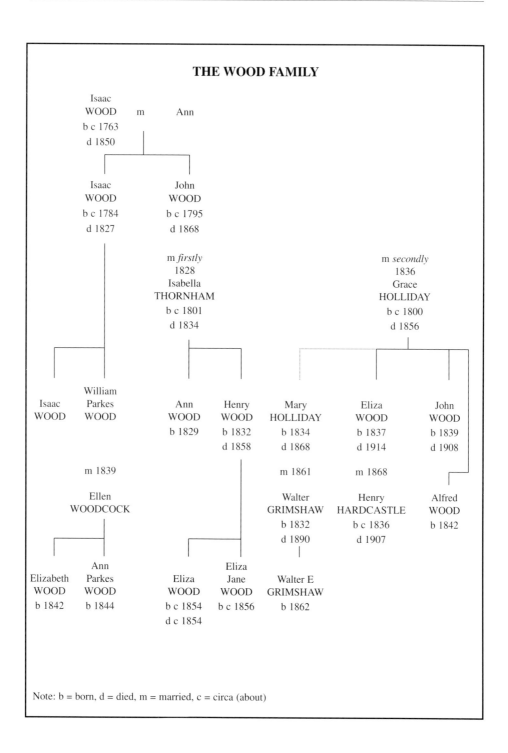

THE WOOD FAMILY

Isaac
WOOD   m   Ann
b c 1763
d 1850

Isaac	John
WOOD	WOOD
b c 1784	b c 1795
d 1827	d 1868

m *firstly*
1828
Isabella
THORNHAM
b c 1801
d 1834

m *secondly*
1836
Grace
HOLLIDAY
b c 1800
d 1856

	William					
Isaac	Parkes	Ann	Henry	Mary	Eliza	John
WOOD	WOOD	WOOD	WOOD	HOLLIDAY	WOOD	WOOD
		b 1829	b 1832	b 1834	b 1837	b 1839
			d 1858	d 1868	d 1914	d 1908

m 1839

m 1861   m 1868

Ellen
WOODCOCK

Walter
GRIMSHAW
b 1832
d 1890

Henry
HARDCASTLE
b c 1836
d 1907

Alfred
WOOD
b 1842

Elizabeth	Ann Parkes	Eliza	Eliza Jane	Walter E
WOOD	WOOD	WOOD	WOOD	GRIMSHAW
b 1842	b 1844	b c 1854	b c 1856	b 1862
		d c 1854		

Note: b = born, d = died, m = married, c = circa (about)

John and Isabella's first child, Ann, was born in 1829 and their second child, Henry, in 1832. In November 1853, when he was 21 years old, Henry Wood opened extensive premises at 13 Low Ousegate with a stock of new jewellery and watches and 'a splendid assortment of unredeemed watches, gold and silver plate' for sale probably partly supplied by his father.[53] He also offered to advance cash to any amount on 'Gold and Silver Plate, Watches, Jewellery, etc'. He was obviously buying and selling the items rather than trading as a pawnbroker, despite the advertisement claiming an office at Lady Peckett's Yard and 'established 80 years'. Henry died in 1858 at the, even for those days, early age of 26, and eighteen months later an advertisement in the *Yorkshire Gazette* offering his stock for sale tried to persuade prospective customers that the articles would be suitable for Christmas presents.[54]

How different were the lives of the sons of the first two pawnbrokers of Lady Peckett's Yard. Richard, the son of George Fettes, did not follow in his father's footsteps and his father allowed him to be declared bankrupt. Henry, the son of John Wood, was helped to set up his own business in a similar line of work to his father. Despite their unequal treatment, both sons traded for about five years, one cut short by debt and the other by death. Yet Richard Fettes had the last word – he later opened a green-grocery business in New York Street, which is now known as Nunnery Lane.

Henry's mother, Isabella, died on 4 October 1834 when he was two years old, possibly while pregnant with her third child. On Christmas Day 1836, John Wood married Grace Holliday at St Crux church and thereby acquired a young step-daughter, Mary.

Parish records show that Mary Holliday was born on 31 March 1834 to Grace Holliday of Bishophill and was baptised four days later at St Mary Bishophill Junior parish in York. There was no mention of who her father might have been. John Wood loved Mary as his own daughter and gave her name as Mary Wood on the 1851 and 1861 censuses of Lady Peckett's Yard. However, Mary was not of the same frame of mind, for when she married Walter Grimshaw of Whitby on 10 October 1861, she signed her name as Mary Holliday and said her father was Thomas Holliday, gentleman.

Walter Grimshaw was born in the West Riding of Yorkshire in 1832, and when he was fourteen years old he was employed as an apprentice to a pawnbroker in York, none other than John Wood.[55] By 1856, Walter had learned the trade and was a pawnbroker in Whitby, returning briefly to York five years later to marry his former employer's step-daughter. Besides being a successful businessman, Walter very much enjoyed playing chess and devising chess problems, rising to the status of President of the York Chess Club. Life became unbearable for him at Christmas time in 1890, for on the morning of Saturday 27 December he committed suicide at his home in Ruswarp, near Whitby, by cutting his throat with a razor.[56] He was buried three days later in Whitby cemetery, aged 58.

In the mid-nineteenth century, the family of pawnbrokers in Lady Peckett's Yard were extremely wealthy, evidenced by the receipt for an enormous family portrait by Thomas Grimshaw of Micklegate which was found with the pledge book and which is illustrated on the next page.

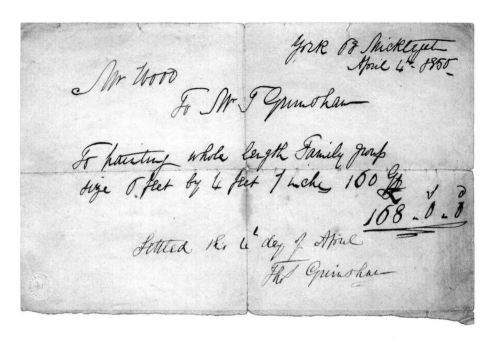

The receipt is dated 4 April 1850 and is for 160 guineas (£168-0s-0d), from Thomas Grimshaw of 68 Micklegate to Mr Wood for painting a whole length family group, size 6 feet by 4 feet 7 inches.

PRICE CARD OF

MR. T. GRIMSHAW,
PORTRAIT PAINTER.

	£. s. d.
8 inches by 7	2 10 0
12 inches by 10	3 3 0
14 inches by 12	4 0 0
17½ inches by 14	5 5 0
21 inches by 17	7 7 0
24 inches by 20	8 8 0
Three quarter, or 25 inches by 30	10 10 0
Kit Cat, or 36 by 28	15 0 0
Small half length, 34½ by 44¾	25 0 0
Half length, 4 ft. 2 by 3 ft. 4	37 0 0
Bishop ditto, 4ft. 8 by 3 ft. 8	46 0 0
Reduced whole length, 4ft. 5 by 5ft. 10	73 10 0
Whole length, 7 ft. 10 by 4 ft. 10	120 0 0
Bishop ditto, 8ft. 10 by 5 ft. 10	150 0 0

Crayon Drawings, £1 and upwards.

Also found was this business card of Mr T Grimshaw, portrait painter, listing his charges from £1-0s-0d for a crayon drawing up to £150-0s-0d for a portrait 8' 10" by 5' 10".

The receipt and the price card were in a small envelope, on one side of which was written 'Granny on Pony; Polly Wood married a Grimshaw; Henry Wood; Uncle John Wood (Boy); Fettes Sword'. Granny would have been Grace, John's second wife (aged about 49), Polly her daughter Mary (16), Henry her step-son and John's son by his first wife (18), Uncle John their joint son (11). Two notable omissions in the portrait are John Wood senior and his daughter Eliza – John commissioned the portrait yet did not wish to be included. The impressive portrait received very favourable public acclaim when it was finished and is now owned by the guild of the Merchant Adventurers in Fossgate, York, where at the time of writing it is on public view.

John Wood senior died on 1 July 1868 aged 73, eleven years after his beloved wife and he had had no difficulty in deciding who should inherit his thriving pawnbroker's business on his demise. He had been successful enough to allow his son, John junior, to live comfortably off his own investments,[57] so for the second time the business was transferred to a man who was not a blood relation, although in this case he was at least an in-law. More than seventeen years earlier, John Wood had employed a young man from Barnsley to help him in the shop and this man had shown great aptitude for the business.[58] In addition, he had taken a fancy to John's youngest daughter, Eliza. That man was Henry Hardcastle.

During the 1840s and 1850s, the pawnbroker's shop in Lady Peckett's Yard could have been mistaken for an introduction agency, for in 1851 both Walter Grimshaw and Henry Hardcastle were working there as apprentice pawnbrokers and they were each eyeing up the owner's daughters. Walter had worked there for five years before Henry was employed, but it was a further ten years before Walter and Mary married. One wonders if there was competition between the two young men and why Walter waited so long to marry. Perhaps he preferred to spend his spare time moving the pawns on the chess board rather than the pawns in the shop.

Henry Hardcastle

Henry Hardcastle was baptised on 21 February 1836 at St Mary's, Barnsley, the same day as his elder brother Charles.[59] He married Eliza Wood, daughter of John Wood, in summer 1868 and they had seven children, all baptised at St Crux where Henry was a churchwarden,[60] the same number as George and Elizabeth Fettes ninety years earlier. Two daughters and a son died during childhood and are commemorated on a family memorial in York cemetery.[61] Also named on the monument are Henry's parents – his mother Sarah died on 18 June 1861 aged 64 years and his father John on 17 March 1866 aged 68 years.

Henry was an excellent business man and he had big ideas for his pawnbroker's business. In 1871, having completed extensive alterations to the premises in Lady Peckett's Yard, which now boasted private offices, he took over the long-established pawnbroker's business of Mrs Rachael Epworth of 6 and 7 Precentor's Court and 102 High Petergate.[62]

H HARDCASTLE (Successor to the late Mr. John Wood), LADY PECKITT'S YARD PAVEMENT, YORK.

PAWNBROKER, SILVERSMITH, JEWELLER, AND GENERAL SALESMAN.

ESTABLISHED 100 YEARS.

TO PERSONS ABOUT TO BORROW CASH.

MONEY ADVANCED at a Reasonable Rate of Interest in Large or Small Sums, on SILVER PLATE, GOLD and SILVER WATCHES, JEWELLERY, Wearing Apparel, Linen, Silks, Books, Beds, Furniture, and every description of Moveable Property. Lots over £10 by Special Agreement.

N.B. – PRIVATE OFFICES.

H.H. having MADE EXTENSIVE Alterations to his Premises, begs to inform the Public of York and the surrounding Districts that he has commenced to RETAIL his UNREDEEMED PLEDGES hitherto sent out of the City for disposal and which consist of GOLD and SILVER WATCHES. Modern and Antique SILVER PLATE, JEWELLERY, WEDDING RINGS, PLATED GOODS, New and Second-hand CLOTHING of every description, BOOTS, and SHOES, BEDS and BEDDING, TABLE LINEN, and a Large and Miscellaneous Collection of Property too numerous to mention.

All Persons favouring H. Hardcastle with a call will find all Goods marked in plain figures, at remarkably LOW PRICES.

NOTE THE ADDRESS – LADY PECKITT'S YARD, PAVEMENT, YORK.

P.S.– GOODS SENT FOR FROM OTHER TOWNS.

Yorkshire Gazette 23 September 1871

He described himself as 'a pawnbroker, silversmith, jeweller and general salesman' and had begun to retail the unredeemed pledges himself rather than disposing of them outside the city as he used to. Pawnbroking in York was then at its peak, with not less than seven pawnbrokers listed in the local directories from 1867 to 1887, and by 1880 Henry and his family could afford to move out of the city centre to the more rural setting of Clifton Green.[63]

Four pawnbroker's assistants were living-in at Lady Peckett's Yard in 1881 and probably also acting as unpaid security guards. Six years later, one of them, Samuel Ernest Haythorn, opened his own pawnbroker's shop, but he did not travel very far. The new shop was at 121 and 123 Walmgate, the next street to Fossgate, despite the fact that the pawnbroker's shop of Henry Calvert in Walmgate had been established for more than fifteen years.[64] Clearly, even one hundred years after the likes of Mary Metcalfe, Alice Cary and Isabella Brown were struggling with their finances, the residents of Walmgate still required the services of a handy pawnbroker or two.

In the mid 1880s, Henry Hardcastle expanded his empire again and took premises at the prestigious site near the Minster on the corner of Stonegate,[65] and by 1893 he had extended the business even further, taking in the adjoining premises in Low Petergate. With its rounded corner, the site was a relatively recent development for York, having been radically improved during 1827 and 1828 because of its being 'the sharpest and most dangerous corner in any of our public thoroughfares, particularly for stage coaches'.[66] At last, Henry had modern premises and occupied one of the most prominent trading sites in York.[67]

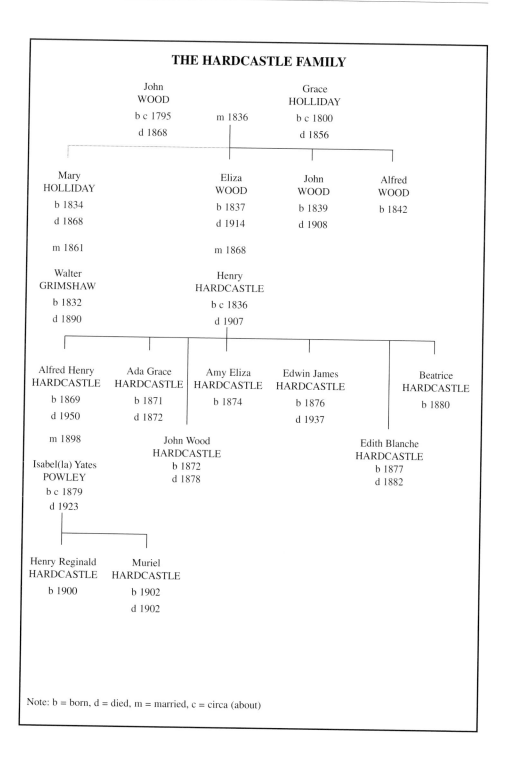

THE HARDCASTLE FAMILY

John
WOOD
b c 1795
d 1868

m 1836

Grace
HOLLIDAY
b c 1800
d 1856

Mary
HOLLIDAY
b 1834
d 1868

m 1861

Walter
GRIMSHAW
b 1832
d 1890

Eliza
WOOD
b 1837
d 1914

m 1868

Henry
HARDCASTLE
b c 1836
d 1907

John
WOOD
b 1839
d 1908

Alfred
WOOD
b 1842

Alfred Henry
HARDCASTLE
b 1869
d 1950

m 1898

Isabel(la) Yates
POWLEY
b c 1879
d 1923

Ada Grace
HARDCASTLE
b 1871
d 1872

John Wood
HARDCASTLE
b 1872
d 1878

Amy Eliza
HARDCASTLE
b 1874

Edwin James
HARDCASTLE
b 1876
d 1937

Edith Blanche
HARDCASTLE
b 1877
d 1882

Beatrice
HARDCASTLE
b 1880

Henry Reginald
HARDCASTLE
b 1900

Muriel
HARDCASTLE
b 1902
d 1902

Note: b = born, d = died, m = married, c = circa (about)

When he died at his home in Clifton Green on 26 November 1907, Henry Hardcastle left an estate valued at over £27,000.[68] Henry and Eliza's eldest son, Alfred Henry, then ran the business for about forty years, probably until the late 1940s, disposing of the original premises in Lady Peckett's Yard some time after 1921.[69] Alfred died just before Christmas 1950 at the Purey Cust Nursing Home in York, which stands to this day in the shadow of the magnificent Minster and about two hundred yards from the site of his business in Stonegate.

Henry Reginald Hardcastle

When Henry Reginald Hardcastle, grandson of Henry Hardcastle from Barnsley and the son of Alfred Henry, took over, he was nearly fifty years old. He not only changed the name of the business but also changed its nature: no longer a pawnbroker's and jeweller's, the business traded as Henry Hardcastle Ltd, antique dealers.[70] In 1949, Henry presented the old pledge book to the City, along with a sword which had belonged to George Fettes during his time as Sheriff.

Thieves broke into the premises in Stonegate/Low Petergate in May 1968 and this may have been a contributory factor when, less than four months later, Henry Hardcastle announced his intention to retire and to move from his home in Strensall near York to live in South Africa.[71] He had became a well-respected businessman and proudly claimed to be a member of the panel of the Worshipful Company of Goldsmiths and a member of the British Antique Dealers Association. He sold his family business to the Leeds-based company of Owen and Robinson Ltd, who, in November 1986, moved out of Stonegate/Low Petergate to Parliament Street, only a stone's throw from where it all began, although the business is no longer there.[72]

George Fettes would have been well pleased that the business which he had developed all those years ago had prospered for so long. A measure of the Hardcastle family's business acumen in moving to Stonegate/Low Petergate is reflected in the asking price for the freehold site when it was for sale in 1988 – no less than £1,600,000, although the adjoining herbalist shop was also included for that sum.

The business may have gone but it is certainly not forgotten, for there are permanent reminders of the earlier times on the shop facades of Stonegate and Low Petergate. Carved above one window of the former shop in Stonegate is 'HENRY HARDCASTLE ESTAB[D] 1770' and under the main windows on the corner of Low Petergate, in large prominent lettering, is 'HARDCASTLE SILVERSMITH JEWELLER'. Few details, if any, survive of the recent patrons, yet much is known of the customers who frequented the pawnbroker's shop more than two centuries ago. We can follow their public lives through parish registers (many printed and indexed), and their private lives through the wonderful old pledge book, listing the items they brought in to Lady Peckett's Yard.

The former Hardcastle premises on the corner of Stonegate and Low Petergate

Lady Peckett's Yard

Appendix A – The Items Pledged

It proved a very difficult endeavour to compile a comprehensive list of the items brought for pledge. As an example, some items were described as 'blue and white' – should this occurrence of 'blue' be included with the total of items described as 'blue', which would give a false and overstated total, or should the 'blue and white' items be totalled separately? Likewise for 'white' items. Another example relates to the total for 'sleeves' – surely the articles described as 'without sleeves' should not be counted in the total for 'sleeves'? And should the total for 'gown' include in it all the bedgowns and nightgowns? The list eventually showed three separate totals for the gowns.

There were other factors to consider, not least the spelling skills (or otherwise) of the pawnbroker and his assistants. For example, calculating a single total for all the pledges adorned with a pattern of flowers was not straightforward – those items were described as 'flowered', 'flowerd', 'flowd', and 'flourd' and the box of artificial flowers had to be excluded from the final total. In order to obtain an accurate total for 'waistcoat' meant realising that the garment was also spelled as 'waist coat', 'waistct', 'waistc', 'waiscoat', 'wascoate', 'wastecoat', 'wast coat' and 'wastcoat'. 'Gold' appeared as 'gould', 'hose' as 'hoes' and so on. Wood-working instruments were spelled in the book as both 'plane' and 'plain', and 'plain' was also used for some items which were unadorned, so judgement had to be applied as to what was the original meaning. In addition, it was sometimes difficult to read exactly what an item was, for example, a shirt or a skirt.

All these factors, and others, meant that it was not sufficient to count (which the computer can do very quickly) the number of times 'blue', for example, occurred in the database, but the pledges had to be scrutinised in great detail. I hope that this resulting list proves useful to the reader and reasonably accurate.

Item or Description	Nr	Item or Description	Nr	Item or Description	Nr
Apron	1,393	Bed ticking	1	Bobbins	2
Artificial flowers	1	Bedgown	85	Body lining	4
Bag	3	Bedside carpet	3	Boiler	1
Baister	1	Bellows	2	Bolster	16
Baize	1	Bib	19	Bolster case	2
Baking pan	1	Bible	19	Bonnet	96
Baking tin	1	Bird net	1	Book	35
Barcelonia	5	Bits (tools)	3	Boot garters	1
Barrow	3	Black	996	Boot legs	1
Basin	5	Blanket	35	Boots	20
Basket	12	Bleached	2	Bottle	1
Bed	6	Blue	102	Bowl	6
Bed curtain	12	Blue & white	8	Box	26
Bed hangings	3	Board	1	Box iron	122
Bed quilt	44	Boat	2	Box iron stand	1

Item or Description	Nr	Item or Description	Nr	Item or Description	Nr
Box rule	1	Chair	1	Cream pot	1
Boys	90	Chair covers	1	Crimson	2
Brace	1	Chamber irons	3	Crown piece	4
Bracket	2	Chania	1	Cruet	1
Brass	29	Check(ed)	699	Cuffs	2
Breadth	3	Child(s)	470	Cup	36
Breast buckle	10	China	15	Curtain	10
Breeches	508	Chintz	4	Damaged	2
Breeds	8	Chisel	2	Damask	18
Bridle	2	Chocolate pot	1	Dark	5
Bristol stone	10	Christening	1	Decanter	2
Broad	3	Cloak	622	Diamond	1
Brocade	1	Cloak lining	1	Dimity	45
Broke	8	Clock	3	Dirty	69
Brown	58	Clogs	3	Dish	35
Bruised	1	Cloth	423	Doeskin	3
Brush	1	Clothes brush	1	Dogskin case	1
Buckle	109	Coarse	134	Double cloth	1
Buckram	1	Coat	931	Double ruffles	3
Buckskin	18	Coating	1	Drab	5
Bunch of willows	2	Coffee mill	1	Drawboy	3
Bundle	7	Coffee pot	7	Drawers (container)	1
Bussey cloth	1	Coin	2	Drawers (wearing)	2
Buttons	58	Common	5	Drawing instruments	2
Calamanca	42	Compasses	1	Drawing tools	4
Callico	1	Copper	16	Dredging box	2
Camblet	6	Corded	7	Dressed (up) cap	17
Cambrick	5	Corduroy	4	Drill (fabric)	6
Can	3	Cork screw	1	Drinking glass	2
Candlestick	28	Corner cupboard	1	Dripping pan	2
Cannister	5	Cotton	693	Duffle	1
Canvas	2	Counterpane	18	Dyed	3
Cap	283	Coverlet	4	Earrings	18
Cap crown	1	Cracked	3	English china	1
Cape	1	Cradle cover	1	English dictionary	1
Cards of lace	2	Cradle lapper	1	Fan	4
Carpet	1	Cradle quilt	2	Feather bed	9
Case	7	Crape	75	Feathers	2
Catcut	1	Cravat	90	Fender	40
Caul	6	Cream boat	9	Figured	19
Chaff	1	Cream jug	8	Fine	23

Item or Description	Nr	Item or Description	Nr	Item or Description	Nr
Fish kettle	1	Hat box	5	Manchester gown	
Flagon	1	Hatchet	3	piece	1
Flannel	70	Heater	52	Manchester made	1
Flannels	1	Hessian	1	Man(s)	213
Flat iron	95	Hipping	4	Mantle	1
Flock	3	Hollows & rounds	1	Measure	1
Flowered	54	Hood	6	Metal	2
Fork	5	Hose	28	Milk pot	1
French	2	Hunters	1	Mitts	7
Frize	11	In pieces	32	Mocketts	1
Frock	200	Irish cloth	10	Mode	43
Fustian	19	Jacket	18	Morter	1
Garden sheers	2	Jam	47	Mourning ring	7
Garnet	9	Japan(ned)	5	Muff	1
Gauges	1	Joseph	1	Muslin	207
Gauze	23	Jumps	6	Nankeen	9
German flute	3	Kersey	5	Napkin	181
Gill	7	Kettle	4	Narrow	7
Gilt	2	Kidd	3	Necklaces	3
Girl(s)	71	Knee buckle	28	Net	28
Glasps	5	Knife/knives	17	New	50
Glazed	1	Knife tray	1	Newspaper	1
Glove(s)	49	Knit	8	Night cap	5
Gold	189	Knitting	2	Night petticoat	1
Gouge	1	Lace(d)	103	Nightgown	8
Gown	1,896	Lamb	2	Nippers	3
Greatcoat	88	Lapper	20	Not finished	2
Green	136	Lappet	3	Oak	5
Grey	21	Lappin	2	Odd	4
Grid iron	2	Large	20	Oil of peppermint	1
Gun	7	Lawn	82	Oil Stone	1
Gunpowder flask	1	Leather	183	Old	1,045
Habit	2	Leeds broad cloth	1	Out of order	1
Hair tin	1	Letter case	1	Oval	1
Hammer	24	Linen	384	Pail	1
Hand bell	1	Lining	9	Pan	15
Hand whip	1	Little	10	Paper bags	1
Handkerchief	1,315	Long	2	Paper box	1
Hank	6	Looking glass	30	Part made	18
Hat	366	Mahogany	6	Paste	4
Hat band	1	Manchester cotton	3	Patten irons	1

Item or Description	Nr	Item or Description	Nr	Item or Description	Nr
Patten leathers	1	Prods	2	Scale	1
Patten woods	3	Prussian	1	Scales	1
Pearl	1	Puder dish	1	Scaneing instruments	1
Pepper box	1	Pumps	11	Scarf	2
Persian	4	Punch ladle	3	Scarlet	89
Petticoat	544	Purple	3	Scotland/Scotch	2
Petticoating	1	Purse	2	Scoop	1
Pewter	66	Quart	2	Screed	4
Picture	3	Quilt	19	Seal	3
Piece(s)/pieced	141	Quilted	154	Seals (or scales?)	1
Pillow	42	Rack	1	Seeing glass	33
Pillow bier	2	Ratteen	1	Serge	3
Pillow case	24	Raw	6	Shag	5
Pillow slip	76	Rawl	1	Shagreen	8
Pin	2	Red	172	Shalloon	12
Pincers	5	Red & white	5	Sheet	268
Pinchbeck	15	Remnant	4	Shift	235
Pinchers	9	Ribbed	5	Shift arms	1
Pincushion	7	Ribbon(s)	47	Shirt	484
Pink	10	Riding habit	2	Shoe buckles	15
Pint	16	Riding hat	1	Shoe upper leathers	6
Plaid	2	Riding skirts	1	Shoes	140
Plain	32	Ring	216	Short	6
Plane	27	Ripped	2	Shovel	18
Plate	38	Robe	1	Sieve	1
Plate stand	2	Robins	2	Silk(y)	904
Plated	57	Round	7	Silver	653
Plow	1	Ruff	17	Silveret	8
Plow plane	1	Ruffled	2	Singlet	3
Plush	5	Ruffles	53	Skin (of animal)	4
Poke	2	Rug coverlet	1	Skirt	181
Pocket bottle	1	Russell	3	Sleeves	189
Pocket handkerchief	10	Russia	8	Slide box	1
Pockets	3	Saddle	1	Slip	10
Poker	19	Saddle strainers	2	Small	203
Pomatum	1	Salt	9	Snuff box	2
Poplin	11	Sash fillister	1	Soiled	3
Prayer book	13	Satin	83	Soup spoon	1
Printed	21	Saucepan	4	Spade	4
Prints	1	Saucer	12	Spoon	37
Prod irons	1	Saw	12	Spotted	7

Item or Description	Nr	Item or Description	Nr	Item or Description	Nr
Sprigged	29	Testament	1	Waistcoat forebodys	1
Spurs	12	Thick set	4	Waistcoat foresides	10
Square	2	Thimble	3	Waistcoating	1
Stays	162	Things	34	Waiter	8
Still	2	Thread	21	Warming pan	6
Still top	1	Tick(y)	2	Wash(ing)	313
Stock	23	Ticket only	4	Watch	197
Stock buckle	13	Tickin(g)	2	Water dishes	1
Stockings	208	Tin	44	Web	2
Stolen	3	Tinder box	1	Weights	1
Stomacher	2	Tobacco box	1	Whip	1
Stone	57	Tongs	33	Whipstock	2
Striped	99	Tooth-drawer		White	556
Strong	4	instrument	1	Wide	3
Studs	1	Tortoiseshell	2	Wig	12
Stuff	413	Towel	11	Window curtain	3
Sugar basin	3	Towelling	1	Wine glass	1
Sugar nippers	1	Trenchers	2	Winemarks	1
Suit of clothes	10	Trimmed	3	Wire	13
Superfine	1	Trunk	2	With one cuff	2
Surtoute	2	Tub	5	Without a lace	3
Susec	1	Tucker	4	Without a lining	12
Sword	1	Tumbler	1	Without an iron	1
Table	1	Turkey stone	1	Without buttons	2
Table vice	1	Un made (up)	105	Without cuffs	6
Tablecloth	179	Unbleached	4	Without sleeves	2
Tablespoon	25	Under blanket	1	Wo(o)lsey	31
Tailors iron	1	Under petticoat	3	Woman(s)	51
Tambour	1	Under waistcoat	3	Wood	2
Tammy	44	Unfinished	4	Wool	2
Tankard	4	Unquilted	2	Wool sheers	1
Tea board	10	Unspun	1	Woollen	11
Tea chest	5	Upper leathers	7	Worked	3
Tea kettle	31	Vallens	1	Worm-eaten	3
Tea table	4	Velvet	19	Worsted	23
Tea tongs	12	Very bad	1	Yarn	18
Tea tray	5	Very coarse	1	Yellow	11
Teapot	4	Very old	8		
Teaspoon	243	Vest	6		
Teaster cloth	1	Waistcoat	741		

Appendix B – The Customers

The surnames of some customers who pledged items appear in the pledge book with several spellings e.g. Norbury, Norbry, Norberry, Noberry or Eyre, Hare. The following list contains the surnames as they were recorded and there has been no attempt to combine names which appear to refer to the same person or family. The columns headed 'Nr' show the number of times a customer with the relevant surname made a pledge, whether for a single item or for multiple items.

Surname	Nr	Surname	Nr	Surname	Nr	Surname	Nr
(missing)	65	Armatage	1	Bails	2	Batty	29
(none)	3	Armitage	6	Bainbridge	4	Baxter	13
...	4	Arnold	1	Bains	2	Baylas	1
...bster	1	Arrundale	1	Bainton	3	Bayles	1
...pkinson	1	Arton	4	Baisting	2	Bayley	1
...son	1	Arundale	9	Bake	11	Bayls	1
...dale	1	Arundell	1	Baker	27	Baynes	1
...shaw	1	Arundill	1	Bakon	1	Bayns	2
...ey	1	Ash	1	Bales	1	Baythorn	2
Abbey	4	Ashburn	1	Ball	1	Baythorne	21
Acron	1	Ashby	4	Balshie	7	Beal	2
Acroyd	2	Ashford	1	Bankhouse	16	Bealby	2
Adcock	1	Ashley	1	Banks	1	Beamont	4
Addey	3	Askwith	1	Bankus	114	Bean	1
Addison	19	Aspenall	1	Bankuss	1	Beane	1
Addy	4	Aspinal	1	Barick	1	Bedall	1
Adinson	4	Aspinall	28	Barker	13	Beeford	23
Adison	6	Aspinwell	1	Barkus	1	Beeforth	146
Alan	1	Astin	1	Barlow	1	Beforth	1
Alanson	9	Atkins	1	Barnes	1	Bell	77
Albert	1	Atkinson	74	Barnet	4	Bellarby	1
Alcock	4	Attar	1	Barnett	6	Bellerby	87
Alford	10	Atter	3	Barret	1	Belwood	3
Alinson	2	Aveson	1	Barrot	1	Benington	1
Allan	4	Awde	2	Barrow	1	Benson	16
Allanson	22	Ayrton	6	Barstow	1	Bentley	8
Allen	4	Ayton	2	Barton	4	Berkenshaw	1
Allinson	1	Backack	1	Bartridge	1	Berkingshaw	1
Allison	3	Backhouse	6	Barwick	2	Berwick	9
Ambler	29	Bacon	1	Bastin	1	Betts	1
Amoss	1	Baghell	1	Bastow	1	Bever	1
Anderson	5	Bagley	1	Batch	1	Bickers	1
Angram	1	Bailes	4	Bateson	2	Biggins	1
Ankins	1	Bailiffe	1	Batteridge	2	Bigings	2

Surname	Nr	Surname	Nr	Surname	Nr	Surname	Nr
Binks	1	Bradburry	5	Bunfield	1	Caulwell	1
Binning	1	Bradbury	9	Burden	3	Caundell	1
Birch	9	Bradley	123	Burdon	1	Cawood	5
Bird	51	Bradshaw	50	Burges	1	Cellars	2
Birdd	1	Braithwaite	6	Burkhead	3	Cellers	2
Birde	1	Braithwate	1	Burnel	1	Chaloner	1
Birkenshaw	3	Bramham	1	Burnell	1	Chambers	13
Birkett	1	Brand	2	Burneston	1	Chandler	1
Birkinshaw	3	Brearah	1	Burniston	1	Chapman	3
Birtch	22	Brearey	1	Burnley	2	Charnick	1
Birth	1	Breary	1	Burton	3	Charnock	4
Blackburn	24	Brerah	1	Busfield	2	Chatem	1
Blackburne	39	Brewer	14	Bussey	13	Cheatam	4
Blaides	1	Brewster	2	Bussie	1	Cheatham	7
Bland	3	Bridgewater	20	Butler	2	Chip	1
Blayds	1	Bridgwater	2	Butt	1	Chipendale	3
Blith	1	Briggs	1	Butter	1	Chipendell	2
Bloxham	1	Brigham	1	Butterfield	1	Chipendill	1
Blunt	1	Bristah	3	Buttery	4	Chipindale	1
Blyth	7	Bristall	3	Buxton	2	Chipindell	1
Blythe	3	Bristoll	1	Cain	1	Chipindill	3
Bocock	2	Brittain	9	Callis	1	Chipingdale	27
Bodwell	1	Broadwell	2	Calvert	13	Chippandale	1
Bointon	1	Brock	1	Camage	1	Chippendale	8
Bonwell	1	Brogden	1	Camidge	7	Chippendell	1
Boocock	12	Brookes	3	Camron	1	Chippindale	1
Bookock	1	Brooks	33	Canady	1	Chippindl	2
Booth	6	Broughton	1	Cant	1	Chippindle	1
Bossell	5	Brown	194	Capen	1	Christian	1
Bossill	1	Browne	1	Capon	3	Clapham	14
Boswell	5	Broxop	1	Carey	55	Clark	22
Botch	4	Broxup	20	Carling	1	Clarke	1
Botham	2	Bruce	1	Carmack	1	Clarkson	38
Boucock	1	Buck	1	Carpenter	1	Clasber	1
Bouls	1	Buckle	9	Carter	1	Clayton	6
Boumer	2	Buckston	1	Cary	17	Clerk	3
Bowcock	1	Budd	14	Casher	1	Clerkson	10
Bower	22	Buddles	1	Cassaday	1	Clewe	1
Bowers	1	Bulfield	4	Cassia	1	Clews	1
Bowling	1	Bullmer	1	Casy	2	Clifford	2
Bowman	13	Bullock	1	Caten	1	Clows	1
Boyd	2	Bulmer	24	Cation	1	Coates	4
Bradbery	1	Bulmire	2	Catton	7	Coats	1

Surname	Nr	Surname	Nr	Surname	Nr	Surname	Nr
Cobb	7	Creaven	1	Davison	1	Dunning	1
Cock	6	Crelles	1	Dawson	21	Durham	1
Cocker	1	Creshaw	2	Day	1	Dyson	18
Coffin	1	Cresser	2	deDeverlans	1	Eadley	1
Coldwell	39	Cressey	2	Dent	6	Eadon	1
Colley	1	Cressor	2	Derby	18	Eaton	3
Collier	59	Crivin	2	Deton	1	Ebbinson	1
Collings	2	Crofft	2	Dibb	4	Ebeson	1
Collingwood	1	Crosland	1	Dickenson	1	Ebetson	1
Collins	4	Cross	1	Dickinson	3	Ebinson	2
Colly	1	Crow	1	Dilman	1	Ebison	2
Collyer	1	Crowder	19	Dimie	19	Eccles	1
Consitt	5	Crowther	8	Dimmie	2	Eckles	4
Cook	7	Croydill	1	Dimmy	2	Edmond	1
Cooke	14	Croysdall	2	Dineley	1	Edmonds	1
Cooper	9	Croysdill	5	Dinsdale	7	Edmondston	1
Corner	1	Crumack	7	Dinsdall	1	Edson	1
Cornett	4	Cryer	2	Dinsdill	2	Edston	2
Cortas	1	Cryke	1	Dixon	58	Edwards	8
Cosens	3	Cuddie	1	Dobson	28	Elinson	1
Cosgrave	2	Cullenworth	2	Dodd	1	Ellett	1
Cossens	5	Cullingworth	2	Dodds	1	Ellise	3
Coton	1	Cundale	22	Dodghson	2	Elton	1
Coulton	1	Cundall	5	Dodgson	1	Emerson	2
Coundale	9	Cundell	2	Dodson	1	English	1
Coundel	1	Cundill	156	Dodsworth	6	Ephraim	3
Coundell	11	Cundle	7	Dollison	1	Ephrakim	1
Coundett	1	Cuningham	1	Doughty	2	Ervin	1
Coundill	3	Cunningam	1	Douglass	11	Eveson	30
Cousens	1	Cunningham	1	Douthwait	1	Evinson	3
Cousins	1	Cusins	1	Douthwaite	2	Evison	2
Coussins	1	Dakeing	1	Douty	2	Eyles	1
Cowper	4	Dakeings	1	Dove	13	Eyre	1
Crabtree	4	Dakin	1	Downs	3	Fairbourn	13
Craft	1	Daking	1	Dowson	5	Fairbourne	8
Cragg	1	Dale	25	Drake	6	Fairburn	1
Craggs	1	Dallyance	1	Droney	2	Fairfoot	1
Crampton	60	Dalton	4	Druket	1	Fairfoott	1
Craven	1	Daniel	5	Ducker	65	Fairguson	1
Creaser	59	Darbishire	2	Duglass	1	Fallowell	1
Creasha	2	Darby	9	Duke	2	Fargason	1
Creashaw	3	Davidson	2	Duning	1	Fargeson	1
Creasor	4	Davis	1	Dunn	1	Farrah	1

Surname	Nr	Surname	Nr	Surname	Nr	Surname	Nr
Farrar	1	Freer	1	Gossup	1	Hardy	15
Farrow	1	Frila	1	Gowland	2	Hare	8
Faucett	1	Frude	2	Gowthorp	1	Harfoot	1
Faulkner	1	Fruide	1	Gradwell	34	Hargate	1
Fawcet	1	Fryer	1	Grainger	1	Hargatt	1
Fawcett	22	Gale	1	Greaves	2	Hargett	1
Fell	10	Garbut	1	Green	78	Hargitt	5
Fenteman	2	Garbutt	1	Greenapple	1	Hargreaves	1
Fentiman	6	Gardiner	10	Greenop	1	Harland	16
Fentimon	1	Gardner	1	Greenside	2	Harley	2
Fentinman	1	Garford	1	Greensides	33	Harr	1
Fillup	1	Gass	1	Greenup	29	Harris	4
Fipson	1	Gauter	1	Greenwood	8	Harrison	150
Firbank	1	Geddins	1	Greeston	1	Harrot	1
Firth	97	Geldard	1	Greevestone	1	Hart	15
Fisher	31	Geldart	1	Greevstone	1	Hartley	4
Flawith	5	Germaine	1	Gregory	2	Harton	6
Flaxton	2	Gibson	40	Griffis	1	Hartt	36
Fletcher	5	Giddings	1	Griffith	1	Hassall	1
Flint	49	Gidins	1	Grimshaw	1	Hast	1
Flinton	1	Gil	2	Gudwell	1	Hatter	37
Flintt	1	Gilbert	4	Haddock	1	Hatton	1
Floweth	1	Gilby	1	Hadlow	7	Haukeswell	1
Flowith	4	Giles	20	Hague	1	Hawkin	1
Flute	1	Gill	15	Hagues	7	Haworth	1
Focett	1	Gillings	1	Hain	1	Haxby	2
Ford	1	Gilson	3	Hair	5	Hay	1
Forsett	1	Girdam	2	Halford	1	Hayes	32
Forth	25	Girdler	8	Hall	31	Hays	7
Foster	2	Girdley	1	Halladay	1	Hayton	1
Fountain	24	Glass	70	Hallfort	1	Headlove	1
Fountaine	84	Glenn	1	Halliday	7	Hebditch	1
Fountane	1	Godson	28	Halliwell	5	Hebtich	1
Fowler	5	Goldthorp	1	Halloday	1	Hebtwitch	2
Fox	3	Goodhale	1	Hallowday	4	Heckler	1
Frame	6	Goodhall	2	Hallowell	8	Helmesley	1
France	7	Goodhil	1	Hammerton	1	Helmsley	22
Frank	5	Goodill	1	Hampson	1	Hemsely	1
Frankland	2	Goodwell	1	Hankins	1	Hemsley	5
Franks	1	Goodwill	1	Harbat	1	Hemsly	2
Frans	1	Goodyear	16	Hardcastle	55	Henderson	5
Frasier	1	Goodyer	1	Hardgrave	3	Hepworth	3
Frazier	1	Gordon	32	Hardgrove	2	Herbert	2

Surname	Nr	Surname	Nr	Surname	Nr	Surname	Nr
Herdsman	6	Hudhnson	1	Kary	3	Leece	1
Heslegrave	1	Hudson	17	Kay	2	Leeting	1
Heslop	2	Hudy	9	Kaye	1	Leng	1
Hessel	1	Hughes	1	Kelsey	4	Lenox	2
Hesslegrave	2	Hulston	1	Kendall	1	Lewise	16
Hewby	2	Hulstone	1	Kendill	1	Lewty	10
Hewson	3	Humphrey	1	Kendrew	4	Lindley	4
Hick	12	Humpleby	14	Kenedy	1	Lindsley	1
Hickman	1	Hunt	2	Kenion	1	Lingley	1
Hicks	1	Hunter	15	Kennedey	1	Linley	2
Hickson	1	Hunton	1	Kennedy	23	Linn	1
Hide	3	Hurst	1	Kennion	2	Linsley	1
Highcrofft	2	Huskins	1	Kershaw	1	Lion	1
Hill	61	Hustler	1	Kershia	2	Lister	1
Hillton	1	Hutchinson	1	Kettlestring	3	Liveridge	1
Hilton	10	Hyde	7	Kettlestrings	2	Liversage	1
Hinderson	3	Ibetson	3	Kidd	1	Liversidge	1
Hindson	2	Idle	1	King	72	Lockwood	3
Hinison	1	Ingleby	1	Kiplin	3	Lofthouse	24
Hipson	2	Ingram	11	Kipling	2	Lomley	5
Hobbott	2	Inman	1	Kirk	3	Lond	1
Hodghson	5	Ireland	3	Kirkman	8	Longley	46
Hodgson	1	Irvin	1	Kitchelah	2	Longly	1
Hodkinson	1	Iveson	4	Kitchinman	1	Longstaff	2
Hog	1	Iyles	1	Kitson	7	Longthorn	6
Holdstock	1	Jackman	3	Knight	1	Longthorne	7
Holford	1	Jackson	95	Knowles	7	Lonley	1
Holloway	1	Jakeman	1	Lacejame	1	Low	3
Holmes	13	James	4	Lambert	1	Lowe	1
Holt	2	Jarmain	1	Langdale	1	Lowson	1
Hop	1	Jebson	2	Langley	4	Lowther	10
Hopkinson	63	Jenkenson	1	Langthorn	4	Lowthorp	1
Hopper	3	Jenkinson	5	Langthorne	1	Luck	4
Hopps	2	Jennings	2	Lasenby	1	Lumley	26
Hops	1	Jephson	6	Lauzanne	1	Lund	12
Hopwood	1	Jepson	1	Lawrence	3	Lupton	5
Hore	1	Jewitt	1	Lawson	2	Lutty	1
Horsley	2	Jiles	1	Lawton	12	Luty	3
Horton	1	Johnson	65	Laycock	1	Lyon	6
Howard	2	Johnstone	1	Lazenby	7	Lyon ?	1
Howe	1	Jowsey	1	Leach	1	Macardy	1
Huby	6	Joy	14	Leatham	1	Mack	1
Huddy	1	Jyess	1	Lee	18	Mackerell	1

Surname	Nr	Surname	Nr	Surname	Nr	Surname	Nr
Mackerill	24	Mills	10	Nailor	3	Orton	7
Mackrell	2	Milner	23	Nayler	4	Ostler	2
Mackrill	3	Milton	2	Neal	1	Otley	1
Made	1	Minter	1	Neale	1	Overton	6
Magill	2	Mires	1	Nelson	1	Owen	4
Maiser	1	Mitchall	1	Newall	2	Owin	1
Manby	3	Mitchell	1	Newcomb	25	Owing	1
Manchester	1	Modehill	1	Newcombe	82	Oxley	1
Mansfield	2	Modersty	1	Newell	1	Pacefull	1
Marling	1	Modesty	31	Newill	8	Pacifull	1
Marshall	24	Modisty	4	Newland	4	Pailer	1
Martin	51	Moiser	13	Newton	5	Palmer	2
Mary (sic)	1	Molam	1	Nichols	2	Pamplin	1
Mason	27	Monk	2	Nicholson	1	Park	1
Massar	1	Moody	2	Nickleson	3	Parker	20
Masser	11	Moor	10	Nickolson	1	Parkin	2
Masterman	4	Moore	158	Nightingale	1	Parkinson	2
Maunby	26	Moorehouse	3	Nightingall	1	Parrott	1
Mawson	9	Moorhead	1	Noberry	1	Pason	1
Maxwell	9	Moorhouse	28	Noble	27	Patrick	3
Mayor	1	Morbry	1	Norberry	2	Pawson	4
Mayson	2	Moreland	2	Norbery	1	Payler	2
Mazeen	1	Moreley	1	Norbry	2	Pears	9
McGill	4	Morell	3	Norburry	6	Pearson	3
Mead	1	Morely	1	Norbury	12	Peck	1
Medcalf	4	Morley	4	Norby	1	Pecket	4
Medcalfe	1	Morrel	1	Norman	4	Peckett	27
Megill	2	Morrell	2	Normandy	1	Peckitt	3
Menhill	1	Morrill	1	Normon	1	Peears	1
Menill	1	Morris	1	Norser	2	Penelton	1
Merriott	4	Morritt	1	North	1	Penington	1
Metcafe	3	Mortimer	1	Nottage	3	Penleton	16
Metcalf	12	Mortus	1	Nursaw	2	Penn	2
Metcalfe	159	Moseley	3	Nurser	31	Pennelton	1
Meyers	1	Moser	1	Nursser	2	Pennington	1
Meynell	2	Motherly	1	Oates	7	Pennleton	1
Micmahon	2	Mountain	2	Oldfield	4	Penrose	36
Middleton	2	Mountfort	1	Oldford	5	Percival	1
Middlewood	1	Moyser	71	Oldridge	1	Perfect	2
Midlewood	1	Mozeen	2	Olford	18	Perkins	1
Millan	1	Mutch	1	Oliver	7	Perry	1
Miller	10	Myers	10	Ollert	1	Petch	10
Millner	1	Nailer	61	Oram	1	Petty	1

Surname	Nr	Surname	Nr	Surname	Nr	Surname	Nr
Philips	1	Pullan	2	Roden	1	Scaley	1
Phillips	8	Pullein	2	Rodgers	2	Scarboro	1
Phipson	3	Pullin	1	Rodwell	9	Scarborough	2
Pick	1	Purdon	1	Rogers	33	Scarbro	16
Pickard	6	Quelch	2	Roper	1	Scarbrough	2
Pickerd	1	Raper	2	Rosewarne	4	Scisand	1
Pickering	1	Raspin	3	Rosewell	6	Scot	1
Pickles	1	Rathmill	1	Rosingdale	1	Scott	47
Piears	1	Raw	13	Rothmill	1	Screven	1
Pindar	25	Rawden	2	Rothwell	14	Screvins	1
Pinder	8	Rawdon	3	Rowe	5	Screwton	14
Plaiser	2	Rawlin	2	Rowel	1	Scriven	8
Plaister	144	Rawlon	1	Rowell	2	Scrivens	2
Plaster	27	Rawson	1	Rowill	2	Scrivin	12
Platt	1	Ray	1	Rowingtine	1	Scrivins	11
Plaxton	2	Reacher	1	Rowley	2	Scrutain	1
Plowman	3	Read	7	Roxwell	1	Scrutaine	1
Plumbe	1	Reader	9	Ruclin	1	Scruton	6
Plumtree	1	Reather	1	Ruclus	27	Scruven	1
Pollard	12	Redford	1	Rucluse	3	Scutain	1
Pollet	1	Reed	26	Rud	1	Seales	1
Pool	2	Render	9	Rudd	196	Seamer	14
Poole	2	Renther	1	Ruddock	1	Seamour	3
Popleton	2	Rhodes	22	Rude	1	Seamur	1
Porter	15	Rice	5	Rummins	1	Sedgwick	1
Portus	1	Richardson	90	Rummons	3	Seemer	1
Potter	5	Richmond	11	Rushton	1	Selby	8
Poultrah	1	Rickaby	2	Russel	1	Sellars	5
Powell	2	Ridsdale	1	Russell	11	Seller	1
Powill	1	Ridsdill	1	Ruston	1	Sellers	59
Preistley	33	Rigby	2	Rut	1	Senior	1
Preistman	4	Riglesby	1	Rutt	1	Seymer	1
Preseman	1	Rigsby	11	Ryley	5	Seymore	2
Preshous	1	Riley	148	Sadler	8	Seymour	9
Preshus	1	Rily	1	Sanderson	5	Shannon	2
Prest	2	Robartson	1	Saunders	1	Sharp	11
Prestman	1	Roberts	1	Savage	1	Shaw	18
Preston	8	Robertson	5	Savall	1	Shawn	1
Prestwich	1	Robins	1	Sawrey	9	Sheaforth	1
Priestley	10	Robinson	94	Scaddlethorpe	1	Shearwood	2
Priestman	3	Robson	9	Scadlethorp	1	Shephard	75
Prince	118	Roculas	1	Scadlethorpe	1	Shepherd	12
Prinse	4	Rodelay	1	Scales	5	Shepperd	1

Surname	Nr	Surname	Nr	Surname	Nr	Surname	Nr
Sherwood	2	Stead	2	Tesseman	28	Varlow	36
Shiphard	1	Steel	2	Tessey	12	Vassa	4
Shipheard	1	Stephenson	4	Tesseyman	3	Vasso	4
Shipherd	2	Sterlin	6	Thew	3	Verd	1
Shiphiard	1	Sterling	2	Thirsk	5	Vincent	1
Shutleworth	1	Stevenson	18	Thomas	11	Viner	6
Shuttleworth	4	Steward	9	Thompson	181	Voner	2
Siddins	1	Stirk	1	Thomson	4	Waddington	3
Silversides	1	Stock	1	Thornley	3	Wadington	12
Simens	3	Storck	1	Thornly	1	Wagill	1
Simmens	5	Stork	41	Thornton	1	Waind	9
Simmons	2	Storke	3	Thorp	1	Waine	1
Simoners	1	Stow	26	Thruth	1	Waineman	2
Simpson	42	Stubb	1	Thue	5	Waite	1
Simson	1	Stubbs	10	Thursk	1	Walace	1
Sisons	1	Stubs	1	Tire	5	Walgate	1
Skelton	15	Sturdy	3	Todd	2	Walise	1
Skilbeck	5	Styan	5	Tomlinson	12	Walker	87
Slaiter	1	Styne	1	Toms	2	Wallis	2
Slater	5	Sugdon	1	Topham	95	Wallise	4
Slator	1	Summer	1	Townley	2	Walls	10
Sledmer	2	Summers	19	Townly	1	Waneman	1
Sledmere	2	Summersett	1	Townsley	6	Ward	1
Sledmire	98	Sunderland	2	Tows	1	Wardall	2
Sleightam	1	Swallow	2	Tunball	1	Wardell	1
Slodard	1	Swan	2	Tunks	3	Wardill	2
Smith	175	Swann	2	Tunsdill	2	Ware	1
Smithson	1	Sykes	4	Tunstill	2	Warren	1
Snow	1	T	1	Turnbull	1	Warwick	1
Snowdon	1	Tail	1	Turner	82	Waters	2
Solitt	1	Tait	2	Turpin	8	Watkinson	18
Sorry	1	Taite	1	Turpine	1	Watley	1
Sotheran	1	Talbot	1	Tutol	1	Watson	28
Southwell	1	Target	1	Twist	3	Wattis	1
Sowrey	1	Tarran	1	Tyne	1	Watts	3
Spencer	29	Tarrant	4	Tyre	1	Waud	7
Spetch	15	Tarrent	3	Umperby	2	Waude	3
Spink	6	Tate	80	Umpleby	5	Wayne	1
Squire	1	Tayler	3	Upton	2	Web	2
Stainer	3	Taylor	1	Urbin	1	Webb	19
Standage	1	Teasdill	1	Vame	1	Webster	49
Starling	1	Tempest	3	Varley	34	Welburn	1
Stayner	2	Tesse	3	Varlo	3	Wellburn	1

Surname	Nr	Surname	Nr	Surname	Nr	Surname	Nr
Wellfoott	1	Whitehill	20	Willson	9	Woodburn	1
Wellford	1	Whithill	1	Wilson	157	Woodhall	13
Wells	1	Whitill	1	Wilstrop	2	Woods	3
Westerman	4	Whitle	5	Wilstrup	1	Wormsley	2
Westland	2	Whitwell	1	Wilton	1	Wray	1
Wheatley	8	Widderington	1	Winer	6	Wright	25
Wheelhouse	2	Wildman	1	Winfield	3	Wrightson	1
Whight	2	Wilford	1	Winn	1	Wyrell	1
Whighthill	1	Wilkins	1	Wirehill	5	Wyrill	1
Whild	1	Wilkinson	13	Wirill	1	Yarrington	1
Whiles	2	Williams	7	Withell	1	Yeoman	2
Whitaker	1	Williamson	2	Witton	1	Yerrington	2
White	54	Willise	1	Wolgate	3	Yessington	1
Whitehall	1	Willison	3	Wood	21	Young	15
Whitehead	20	Wills	1	Woodall	1		

Appendix C – Where the Customers Lived

In the pledge book there were marked differences in the spellings of the places which the customers called home, which was hardly surprising since street names did not begin to be fixed to street corners in York until 1782.[73] 'Goodramgate' was also 'Goderhamgate' and 'Gudram Gate', even apparently simple words like 'Lane' became 'Lain', and there were very many such discrepancies. The spellings were entered on the computer database exactly as they had been written, so in order to facilitate analysis and totalling, an extra field was added to contain a standardised spelling of the place name or, where a street had been renamed over the intervening years, the current street name. The only exceptions were the three Water Lanes, which retained their original names on the computer so that they could be listed in this section next to each other.

In the Pledge Book	Current Name
Girdlergate	Church Street
Thursday Market	Saint Sampson's Square
Jubbergate	Jubbergate and Market Street
First Water Lane	King Street
Middle Water Lane	Cumberland Street
Far Water Lane	Friargate

Several present-day streets of York had not been constructed at the time of the pledge book e.g. Clifford Street, Piccadilly, Parliament Street and neither had the bridges across the River Ouse at Skeldergate, Lendal and Clifton. There were ferries, but these made a charge, so the most usual river crossing into York city centre from the south or west would have been across Ouse Bridge, which itself was rebuilt and reopened in 1820. The Skeldergate and North Street of today would be largely unrecognisable to the citizens of the eighteenth century – the small houses and wharves have been demolished and in their places are warehouse conversions and luxury flats, even hotels. These are all highly sought after now because of their attractive river frontage, but are slightly less desirable when the River Ouse floods, which the former citizens of York would certainly have known about.

Among the more unusual places where the customers lived were:

Place as Written	Corrected Spelling
Coppen Thorp	Copmanthorpe
Easeingwould	Easingwold
Foulforth	Fulford
Jelly Gate	Gillygate
Mazendew	Maison Dieu
Nuton upon Derwin	Newton upon Derwent
Old work	Aldwark
Wheatherby	Weatherby
Yeswick	Earswick

Current Address	Nr	Current Address	Nr
(Address not readable)	28	Castlegate Postern	4
(Deaf woman)	10	Castlegate Postern, out of	1
(No address given)	30	Castlegate, at Mr Agars	1
(Part of page missing)	43	Castlegate, at The Wheatsheaf	1
(Travelling woman)	1	Castlegate, Church Lane	13
Acaster	4	Castlegate, Church yard	2
Acaster Malbis	1	Castlegate, Hospital	1
Acklam	1	Church Street	161
Acomb	14	Church Street, at Mrs Graves	1
Aldwark	167	Church Street, Three Cranes	1
Aldwark, at Flints	1	Clifton	42
Aldwark, at George Marshalls	3	Coffee Yard	11
Aldwark, at Mrs Walkers	1	Colchester	1
Allerton Mauleverer	4	College Street	26
Army, 11th Regiment	1	Colliergate	91
Army, 11th Regiment of		Coney Street	69
Dragoons	1	Coney Street, at Mr Barritts	1
Army, Johnston's Dragoons	1	Coney Street, at Mr Coles	1
Askham Bryan	1	Coney Street, at The Black Swan	2
Baildon near Bradford	1	Coney Street, at The George Inn	4
Barker Lane	52	Coney Street, Church Lane	1
Barwick	1	Coney Street, Judges Lodgings	9
Barwick near Aberford	1	Copmanthorpe	4
Bedale, near	2	Coppergate	144
Bedern	35	Coppergate, at Heels	1
Beverley	1	Coppergate, at The Horseshoe	1
Bilton	1	Cottingworth	1
Bishophill	188	Davygate	57
Bishophill Junior	6	Derby	1
Bishophill, at Kingpipins	1	Doncaster	2
Bishopthorpe	4	Driffield	1
Bishopthorpe, Queens Head	1	Dringhouses	6
Blake Street	1	Duncombe Place	4
Blossom Street	3	Duncombe Place, at Osterfields	1
Bootham	39	Dunnington	11
Bootham Bar	8	Earswick	8
Bootham Bar, near	1	Easingwold	2
Bootham Bar, out of	1	Ebberston near Malton	1
Bramham	3	Escrick	4
Bridge Street	17	Feasegate	171
Carlton Husthwaite	1	Fenton near Sherburn	1
Castle Mills	14	Fishergate	2
Castlegate	24	Foss Bridge	43

Current Address	Nr	Current Address	Nr
Foss Bridge Hospital	10	Lincoln	1
Fossgate	593	London	2
Fossgate, at Boltons	1	Low Wortley near Leeds	2
Fossgate, at George Grays	1	Maison Dieu	3
Fossgate, at Jane Newcombs	10	Malton	10
Fossgate, at Sellers	1	Marygate	58
Fossgate, Greenwood Yard	1	Medley near Leeds	1
Fossgate, Merchant Adventurers Hall	6	Melton near Hull	1
Fulford	83	Micklegate	293
Gillygate	23	Micklegate Bar	39
Goodramgate	203	Micklegate Bar, near	1
Goodramgate Church Yard	27	Micklegate Bar, out of	9
Goodramgate, at Silcocks	1	Micklegate Bar, without	1
Goodramgate, at Susannah Wallis	1	Micklegate, at Mattersons	1
		Micklegate, at Mr Arthingtons	2
Grape Lane	16	Micklegate, at Mr Earbys	1
Great Askham	1	Micklegate, at Mr Hagues	1
Helmsley	1	Micklegate, at The Artichoke	1
Heslington	10	Micklegate, at The Falcon Inn	1
Holgate	2	Middleton Tyas near Richmond	1
Holgate Road	15	Minster Yard	11
Holtby	1	Mint Yard	7
Hornpot Lane	9	Monk Bar	57
Hull	1	Monk Bar, at Barnetts	3
Hungate	254	Monk Bar, out of	11
Hungate, at Betty Doves	1	Monk Bar, out of, at Blyths	1
Hungate, at Mrs Hoggitts	1	Moor Monkton Parish	1
Huttons Ambo	1	Mount, The	1
Jubbergate	365	Naburn	6
Jubbergate, at Hawkeswell House	4	Naburn Mill	1
		Nessgate	2
Jubbergate, at Three Cranes	1	New Street	1
Jubbergate, at Three Swans	1	Newcastle under Lyme	1
Kelfield	1	Newgate	76
Kilburn	23	Newton on Derwent	9
Kings Square	1	Newton on Ouse	1
Knapton	2	North Dalton	1
Knaresborough	4	North Street	1,291
Knottingley	2	North Street Church Yard	60
Leeds	5	North Street Postern	6
Lendal	34	North Street Postern, out of	28
Lendal, at Bluitts	1	North Street, at Martha Shephards	1

Current Address	Nr	Current Address	Nr
North Street, at Mr Hopps	1	Saint Saviourgate	90
North Street, out of	1	Scarborough	2
Ogleforth	10	Scrayingham	1
Ouse Bridge	100	Selby	1
Ouse Bridge Jail	19	Settle	1
Ouse Bridge, other side of	5	Shambles	275
Ouse Bridge, other side of, at		Shambles, Little	94
Perrys	5	Sheffield	1
Ousegate	5	Sheriff Hutton	1
Ousegate, High	1	Silver Street	11
Ousegate, Low	22	Silver Street, at Dixons	2
Patrick Pool	1	Skeldergate	470
Pavement	62	Skeldergate Postern, out of	2
Pavement, Bellyard	1	Skeldergate, Middletons Hospital	16
Pavement, Hosier Lane	2	Skipton in Craven	1
Pavement, Tollhouse	2	Snaith	1
Peasholme Green	57	Sowerby near Thirsk	1
Peter Lane	263	Spurriergate	54
Peter Lane, at Mrs Briggs	1	Stillingfleet	4
Peter Lane, Little	33	Stockton	4
Petergate	468	Stonebow Lane	3
Petergate, High	16	Stonegate	32
Petergate, Low	29	Stonegate, at Mr Baldocks	3
Petergate, Low, at Bulmers	1	Stonegate, at The Starr	1
Petergate, Racketts	12	Sutton in Ashfield	1
Pocklington	4	Sutton near Tadcaster	2
Pontefract	2	Sutton on Derwent	1
Poppleton	2	Sutton on Forest	1
Precentors Court	3	Sutton on Forest, Sutton Carr	1
Pump Yard	4	Swine market	2
Queens Staith	1	Swinegate	259
Richmond	1	Swinegate, at Francis Taylers	1
Richmond, Garriston	1	Tadcaster	18
Saint Andrewgate	31	Tadcaster or Leeds	1
Saint Helens Square	3	Tadcaster, near	1
Saint Martins Lane	2	Tanner Row	42
Saint Maurices Road	4	Tanner Row, at The Grey Horse	1
Saint Michael le Belfrey parish	1	Tanner Row, Nursery House	167
Saint Sampsons Square	206	Tower Street	2
Saint Sampsons Square, at The Royal Oak	2	Towthorpe	1
		Trinity Church Yard	11
Saint Sampsons Square, at Woodhalls	1	Trinity Lane	37
		Walmgate	1,156

Current Address	Nr	Current Address	Nr
Walmgate Bar	54	Water Lane, at Mr Derbyshires	1
Walmgate Bar, out of	38	Water Lane, Far	198
Walmgate, at Brothertons	1	Water Lane, Far, at Francis	
Walmgate, at Joseph Holmes	1	Hodgsons	1
Walmgate, at Mr Acroyds	1	Water Lane, Far, at Mr Pitts	1
Walmgate, at Peggy Vassos	1	Water Lane, First	361
Walmgate, at The Cross Keys	1	Water Lane, First, at Lumleys	7
Walmgate, Church Yard	1	Water Lane, First, at Molly	
Walmgate, George Street	1	Harrisons	1
Walmgate, out of	1	Water Lane, Middle	152
Walmgate, Saint Denys	1	Water Lane, Middle, at The	
Walmgate, Saint Denys Church		White Bear	1
Yard	16	Water Lane, Middle, Cross Alley	4
Walmgate, Saint Margarets		West End near Otley	1
Church Yard	4	Wheldrake	1
Walmgate, Saint Margarets		Wigan	1
parish	1	York	8
Warthill	3	York Castle	29
Water Lane	513		

Appendix D – The Watches Pledged

The list which follows shows all the watches which were pledged where the manufacturer was noted – most were listed in the pledge book with the name of the manufacturer and the serial number. The pledges are listed as they were spelled in the pledge book, along with the number of days each was in the care of the pawnbroker. Watches with an entry of '-' under 'Days' were not redeemed. The assistant pawnbrokers found it difficult to spell the makers' names correctly even when all they had to do was copy them from the watches, although the gloom of a winter's day might be used in their defence on some occasions.

Watch Maker & Watch Number	Days	Watch Maker & Watch Number	Days
Jno Agar York 385	3	Fs Coulton York 4753	3
John Agar York 405	2	Silver watch 4753	-
Seth Agar York	-	J Dale London 2535	-
Jno Akced London 1855	19	Jno Dann Dearham 1800	7
Dan Atkins 18797	-	Jno Darby London 10356	2
Barlow London 21036	64	Geo Darvill London 1267	42
J Barrow	26	Wm Dent London 3907	-
J Barrow	7	P Deslauny Paris 585…	15
J Barrow	9	R Deslaunys Paris 5852	-
Wm Barton London 7299	-	Thos Doncaster Wigan 506	54
H Bieres	-	Robert Doore London	128
D Bowly London 740	-	Robt Doore London	61
Britley London 225	-	D Edmonds Liverpool 511	2
Jas Brogden London 46…	-	Jno Edmonds London 1015	-
Jere Bromby London 740	-	Jno Edmonds London 3823	-
Saml Burgis London	-	Jno Edmonds London 3893	39
Wm Burnett London 15390	-	Jas Edwards Corke 4191	1
F Butt London 911	-	Jas Edwards Corke 4191	118
J Butts London 911	88	Jas Edwards Corke 4191	96
Wm Byfield London 3137	28	Jas Edwards Corke 4191	129
C Cabrier London 5407	11	James Edwards Corke 4191	118
Ja Campbell London 4242	50	Jno Etherington London 40	91
Jas Chambers London 150	1	Jno Etherington London 40	3
J Charleson London 6556	109	Jno Evereds London 6320	16
Wm Clark York 2	191	Richd Finch London 105	-
C Clay London 2554	248	Richd Freber London 2267	-
J Clayton London 2187	-	Thos French Norwich 1677	5
Thos Collings Doncaster	15	Jno Gardiner London	-
John Cook London 607	-	B Glover London 2942	9
Frans Coulton York 4753	41	Wm Gold London 8	110
Frs Coulton York 4753	5	Wm Gold London 8	84

Watch Maker & Watch Number	Days	Watch Maker & Watch Number	Days
Chas Goode London	7	Langley	-
Chs Goode London	26	A Le Roy Paris	38
Willm Gordon London 3279	-	Mr Le Roy Paris	38
Grant London 882	9	Gilbt Lloyd London 1753	112
Wm Grant London 2406	84	Wm Love London 13779	154
Wm Grant London 6982	-	D Manley London 3886	38
Grimes London 3214	-	Char March London 259	3
Thos Hally London 329	164	Chs Markwick London 1197	93
Jno Hardin London 1333	-	Chars Marsh London 259	30
J Harris London	59	Edwd May Witney	269
J Harris London 1363	-	Geo Meakins London 345	123
Hart Bristol 3296	36	Geo Meakins London 345	-
D Heddon London 3524	68	Millington London 4198	63
Edwd Hemman London 3879	53	Millington London 4198	-
Robert Higgs London 2632	1	Moore London 1525	-
Jonas Hill York 8732	14	Moore London 5277	193
H Hindley York 1938	91	T Moore London 3886	21
James Hirst London 5300	88	C Morin London 1306	28
Amil Hobech London 43	-	R Motley London 169	109
Wm Holmes London 1765	4	R Motley London 169	3
William Holmes London 1765	105	R Motley London 169	7
Wm Howard London 6652	1	Jas Newton Guernsey 8515	35
Wm Howard London 6652	858	Jno Noldar London 56	23
Wm Howard London 9912	83	Ogden 4154	139
Wm Howard London 9912	34	Ogden 4154	96
Wm Howard London 10032	52	James Ovingham London 1296	-
T Hulett London	1	Robt Ovingham London 12909	12
Benjne Hutchinson London	-	Richd Parker London 5238	77
Wm Jackson Thirsk 178	14	John Pepys London	34
Matt Jarvis Dalton	247	Francis Pinne London 15949	-
J Johnson Liverpool 1001	0	M Ransom London 8438	-
Jno Jonson London	4	M Ransom London 8875	-
T Josel London 281	9	John Reiley Dublin 173	1
Josephson London 8087	-	James Reith Versailles 220	1
Josephson London 16515	4	Thos Reynolds Warwick 364	-
Josephson London 16515	358	J Richards London 22014	1009
D Keddin London 3524	14	J Richards London 22110	8
T Kellett London	6	J Richards London 22110	63
Wm Kellewey Chelmsford	-	J Richards London 22424	1
S Knutsford Wavertree	-	J Richards London 22609	68
J Land London 406	26	J Richards London 24022	71
Wm Land London 1500	17	J Richards London 26030	-

Watch Maker & Watch Number	Days	Watch Maker & Watch Number	Days
Jno Ritcher London	4	Sam Towlam London 1524	-
Thos Sampson London 3596	-	J Tringham London 17884	100
P Sellars London	-	J Tringham London 17884	-
Jno Shaw Holburn 3063	-	Jos Turgees London 1777	-
Robt Skinner London 1487	145	Jos Turges London 1777	89
Robt Skinner London 1487	110	Rt Walker London 7901	188
Jno Smith Dublin 2520	1	Jas Watts London 5846	1
Jno Smith Yk 102	183	Weldon London 5641	1
Jno Smith York 172	8	Weldon London 5641	148
Jos Smith London 163	-	Weldon London 5641	-
Samuel Spurrier 7293	86	Jas Williams London 100	161
Edwd Stem London 1620	3	R Williamson Royal Exchange	210
B Storr	269	Jno Willis London 210	96
Batty Storr York	96	Jno Willis London 210	0
Marm Storr London 9069	18	G Wilson London 1101	37
Marmke Storr London 9069	320	Jno Wilson London 3492	15
Wm Success London 489	80	J Windmill London	5
Wm Sucess London 489	113	Peter Wise London	242
Jno Tenybel London	-	Wm Worcester London 2985	1
Saml Toulman London 1524	15	Jno Wright London 2971	-
Saml Toulman London 1524	49	... field Bath 3097	2
Saml Toulman London 3294	18		

Appendix E – Types of Clothing

During the eighteenth century, there were no clothes shops as we understand them today. Garments were made individually, either made-to-measure (if one could afford it), or, for the vast majority of people, they were handed down from person to person and altered to give a better fit. The books available today which depict the fashions of those times tend to concentrate on the attire of the well-to-do citizen, largely because their clothes were the ones which survived the rigours of time, due to their being better made and handled more carefully and perhaps even being worn by fewer people.

The patrons of the pawnbroker in Lady Peckett's Yard would have been unable to keep up with the latest fashions, so clothes which were old or unfashionable would have had to be worn. The following list is restricted to items which were actually pawned at the York shop and is therefore what the ordinary people of York wore. The bibliography recommends books for further reading about the fashions of the time.

Item	Description
Apron	Made with a running string at the waist which could be gathered in as desired and tied at the back. They were of varying lengths and colours and made of lawn, muslin, gauze, crape, net, silk or satin, often edged with lace or embroidered
Barrow	A simple garment worn by an infant for warmth. Usually of flannel and like a long blanket with tucks at the waist and tied at the back
Bodice	The top part of a dress
Bonnet	A hat, probably with ribbons to tie under the chin
Breeches	Leg coverings usually ending just above or below the knees
Cap	Indoor wear with lace, ribbons or frills. A hat or bonnet would have been worn on top when going out
Cravat	A band of material such as linen or lawn, worn round the neck with the ends tied loosely under the chin in a knot or bow
Frock	A gown for a child. Also, a coat for informal wear with a turned down collar
Gloves	Often elbow length and mainly worn only on dress occasions
Greatcoat	A long loose overcoat with a flat collar and a smaller collar above
Half-handkerchief	Half a square handkerchief, cut diagonally
Handkerchief (men)	Lawn or cambric handkerchiefs were edged with lace for display and often scented. Silk ones, often very ornamental, were used by snuff takers

Item	Description
Handkerchief (women)	The most general form of neck covering during the second half of the eighteenth century and varied in size, shape, colour and material. In the 1770s, handkerchiefs were large and draped round the neck and shoulders, where they were often secured by pinning. The long ends were either left to fall loose in front or were worn fastened with a brooch or threaded through a ring
Jam	A frock worn by a child
Joseph	A woman's long riding cloak
Jump	Another name for stays
Lappets	Pendants on indoor headwear either hanging at the back or sides
Nightgown	Un-boned loose dress worn informally for comfort, but not as night attire
Petticoat	A garment worn under an open overskirt. It was meant to be seen and was often highly decorated
Pockets	Small bags attached to a tape and worn round the waist beneath a skirt, reached through an opening in the skirt. Separate items, usually in pairs
Robings	Flat trimmings or border around the neck and down the front of a bodice. Sometimes down the edges of an open overskirt
Ruff	A starched circular collar radiating from the neck
Ruffles	Detachable decorative cuffs
Shift	A loose fitting garment of linen worn next to the skin
Sleeves	A pair of sleeves could be worn over the sleeves of another garment to protect the garment.
Stays	A corset stiffened with whale-bone to improve the wearer's figure and deportment
Stock	A high stiffened neck cloth fastened behind with a buckle
Stomacher	Triangular stiffened material used as a fill-in for an open bodice, sometimes embroidered or jewelled
Tucker	White frilled edging to a low-necked bodice, or a kind of bib
Waistcoat	A sleeveless jacket with the front made of better fabric than the back. Usually worn under a frock or coat
Waistcoat sleeves	Sleeves could be added to a waistcoat for warmth

Appendix F – Types of Fabric

Fabric	Description
Bays or Baize	A coarse open woollen fabric with a plain weave
Bombazet	An inferior imitation of bombazine
Bombazine	A slight twilled textile of cotton and worsted. Used in mourning and generally black
Calamanco	A glossy woollen fabric, chequered or brocaded in the warp
Calico	A cotton textile
Cambric	A fine French linen
Camlet	A stuff originally made of camel's hair and later made of wool and silk
Chintz	A glazed calico with pattern painted or printed in colours
Corduroy	A stout corded cotton with a pile like velvet
Crape	A thin silk gauze, crimped
Damask	A figured fabric of silk or linen
Dimity	A stout cotton fabric with a ribbed surface
Drab	A thick woollen cloth of a yellowish colour
Drawboy	A fine figured material
Figured	Marked with figures or designs
Fustian	A coarse twilled cloth with linen warp and cotton weft
Gauze	A very thin silk or cotton
Irish cloth	With a silk warp and worsted weft
Kersey	A coarse cloth
Lawn	A very fine linen
Linen	A cloth made from flax
Manchester cotton	A textile with stripes of cotton and wool
Muslin	A fine thin cotton cloth
Nankeen	An Indian cotton textile of a yellowish brown colour
Ratteen	A kind of coarse woollen stuff, quilted or twilled
Satin	A silk twilled textile with a smooth glossy surface
Shalloon	A slight woollen stuff
Silk	A fine lustrous material made from thread produced by silk-worms
Stuff	A woven textile usually of common wool, which was plain or twilled
Tammy	A plain piece of long-stapled wool
Towelling	A thick linen cloth
Twilled	A fabric woven to produce diagonal ribs
Woolsey	A coarse fabric made from wool and cotton
Worsted	A fine, woollen fabric, closely woven, made from yarn spun out of long, combed wool and used for hard-wearing garments

Appendix G – Other Items and Terms in the Pledge Book

Item or Term	Description
Bed	A feather mattress
Bolster	A long round pillow
Box iron	An item used to smooth out creases but with a small chamber in it where a pre-heated slug of metal could be inserted (a heater), thus ensuring the base of the iron remained clean. Ironing could proceed more quickly if there were two or more heaters
Clogs	Wooden soled shoes
Counterpane	A bed covering
Fender	A fence to keep in the cinders of a fire
Fillister	A plane for grooving
Flat iron	An item used to smooth out creases and heated on a fire
Gill	A container for a quarter of a pint of liquid
Glasp	A device (like a hook) for holding objects or parts together
Heater	Used inside a box iron
Hipping	A napkin wrapped about an infant's hips
Hollows and rounds	Tools used by a carpenter
Intaglio	A form of engraving or carving, in which the pattern or design is sunk below the surface of the material (opposite of cameo)
Japanned	Made black and glossy with hard varnish
Napkin	A piece of material (either cloth or paper) used at table to wipe the lips or fingers and to protect the clothes, or a small cloth or towel
Pattens	Wooden overshoes on a high iron rung. They were used in muddy or dirty streets to raise the shoes out of the grime
Pinchbeck	A yellow alloy of copper and much less zinc than ordinary brass, simulating gold. It denoted bad quality and falsity and was used a lot for watch cases
Poke	A bag or pouch
Pomatum	Perfumed lubrication for the hair, often made of hog's lard or sheep suet
Pumps	Low shoes with thin soles, used for dancing
Shagreen case	These were often used for watches and were made of fish skin
Tea kettle	It stood on a spirit burner on the table to make a drink of tea
Tinder box	Used to make a spark to light a fire
Trencher	A wooden plate
Waiter	An indoor portable carrying device with two or three tiers
Watch	Two were frequently worn from the 1770s to the early 1780s but one was sometimes a sham. A very fashionable item

Appendix H – The Spinning School

The following table is included to allow a comparison to be made with the items pledged at the pawnbroker's shop in Lady Peckett's Yard.

In about 1782, twenty-two young girls were entered into a newly formed Spinning School in the centre of York. The school's stated ideal was 'to excite a spirit of virtuous industry among the children of the poor'. The girls were taught to read, knit and sew in the evening after they had finished their work of spinning worsted and they attended public worship twice each Sunday. By about 1785, the girls were provided with the following items of clothing, usually made by themselves, in proportion to their labour.

Spinners from four to six Hanks a day.	*Six Hanks. In Addition.*	*Seven Hanks. Additional.*	*Eight Hanks. Additional*
A stuff Gown. Two linen Bedgowns. Two Shifts. Two pair of Shoes. Two checked handkerchiefs. Two blue Aprons. A Straw Hat. Two pair of Stockings. Three ounces of Worsted. Shoes mended twice. 1 Wolsey Petticoat.	A checked Apron.	A Cap. A coloured Shawl. A pair of Pattens.	A Green Riband round the Hat. A pair of Worsted Mittens.

Spinners of Ten Hanks. Additional.	*Eleven Hanks. Additional.*	*Twelve Hanks. Additional.*
A better Shawl. A Wolsey Petticoat. One Shift. One White Apron.	One Cap. A Stuff Petticoat with the Gown.	One checked Apron. A Black Bonnet.

Stays were allowed to those girls who had regularly spun seven hanks per day for one year. Cloaks were lent, not given, to the girls, but they were allowed to keep them when they finally left the school providing they had behaved well enough.[74]

Appendix I – The Currency

Decimal currency was not introduced in England until 1971. In the 1770s, the English monetary system was based on 12 pennies in a shilling and 20 shillings in a pound. The most common coins available were as follows:

Coin	Meaning
¼d	Quarter of a penny, known as a farthing
½d	Half a penny, pronounced hay-penny
1d	One penny
3d	Three pennies, pronounced thru-pence or thre-pence
4d	Four pennies, or a groat
6d	Six pennies, pronounced six-pence
1s-0d	One shilling, later often written as 1/-
2s-6d	Two shillings and six pence, or half a crown
5s-0d	Five shillings, or a crown

A guinea was £1-1s-0d, two guineas was £2-2s-0d, twenty guineas was £21-0s-0d and so on.

Selected Bibliography

G H Baillie *Watchmakers and Clockmakers of the World* (London 1947).
C Willett Cunnington & Phillis Cunnington *Handbook of English Costume in the Eighteenth Century* (Faber & Faber Ltd 1972).
Kenneth Hudson *Pawnbroking - An Aspect of British Social History* (The Bodley Head 1982).
Josephine Kamm *The Hebrew People* (Victor Gollancz Ltd 1967).
Brian Loomes *Watchmakers and Clockmakers of the World Volume 2* (London 1976).
Jonathon Magonet *The Explorer's Guide to Judaism* (Hodder & Stoughton 1998).
Marion Sichel *Costume Reference 4 - The Eighteenth Century* (B T Batsford Ltd 1977).

[1] *The Living Bible*, Deuteronomy 24:6 & 17 (Tyndale House 1990).

[2] *An Inventory of the Historical Monuments in the City of York – Volume V The Central Area* (Royal Commission on Historical Monuments, London 1981), page 152.

[3] 8 October 1778 on three tickets.

[4] Redeemed 10 April 1778.

[5] John McGill of Hungate, 7 October 1777 with a pair of yarn stockings, 2s-4d, unredeemed, sold 14 August 1778.

[6] Mary Bowman of Peter Lane, 15 August 1777, 6d, redeemed on the same day.

[7] Eliz Harrison of Feasegate, 15 September 1777, 1s-6d, redeemed 16 March 1778.

[8] Mrs Tate of Swinegate, 28 November 1777, 3s-6d, redeemed 2 December 1777.

[9] Mary Wilson of Bishophill, 4 November 1778, 6d, redeemed 6 November 1778.

[10] 3 September 1778, redeemed 16 November 1778.

[11] 14 October 1778 with an old waistcoat also, total 4d, redeemed 17 November 1778.

[12] 21 July 1778, 10d, redeemed 4 August 1778.

[13] 14 December 1778, 1s-8d, apparently unredeemed.

[14] 3 October 1778, 2s-0d, redeemed 23 October 1778.

[15] 11 September 1778, 12s-0d, redeemed 26 September 1778.

[16] 20 September 1777, unredeemed.

[17] 5 August 1777, redeemed 23 October 1777.

[18] 30 May 1778, redeemed 22 June 1778.

[19] Thursday 14 August 1777.

[20] Abode missing, 26 September 1778, redeemed 20 October 1778.

[21] 29 November 1777, unredeemed.

[22] 5 August 1777, 1s-6d.

[23] 14 July 1777, 1s-6d.

[24] 2 August 1777 and 6 November 1777, for 1s-0d each.

[25] 23 October 1777, redeemed 24 February 1778.

[26] *Yorkshire Gazette*, 16 October 1778, page 1.

[27] *York Courant*, 16 March 1779, page 2.

[28] 31 July 1777, not redeemed.

[29] 25 October 1777, not redeemed.

[30] 4 May 1778, 27 June 1778, 1 August 1778, all redeemed.

[31] 12 September 1778, redeemed 9 October 1778.

[32] *York Courant*, 19 July 1774, page 3.

[33] Baptism Register of St Crux, 14 July 1784.

[34] *York Courant*, 5 March 1810, page 2.

[35] *Dictionary of National Biography* (published 1888-9, reprinted 1949-50), Volume 6, page 1259, and *The Times*, 1 July 1836, page 4.

[36] CYA *York Apprenticeship Registers*, D14 (Appr 1756 - 1786), page 199.

[37] CYA *Chamberlain's Account Books*, Volume 75, page 7.

[38] CYA *Chamberlain's Account Books*, Volume 59, page 6.

[39] Wm Parson & Wm White, *Directory of the Borough of Leeds, the City of York etc* (1830), page 314.

[40] Burial Register of St Crux, 4 February 1831.

[41] CYA House Book B46, 27 November 1802, pages 424 - 425.

[42] CYA House Book B46, at the back of the book, lists the attendances of commoners and gentlemen of the Twenty four, continuing into B47 and B48, whereupon the list ceases. George Fettes' first attendance was on 15 January 1798 and his final one listed was 9 May 1828.

[43] W Camidge, *York Savings' Bank* (1886), pages 26 and 103.

[44] Reproduced from an original in the Borthwick Institute (BIHR), University of York, Prog George Fettes of York November 1831, Prog Elizabeth Fettes of York November 1831.

[45] Oliver A Beckerlegge, *John Wesley comes to York* (No publisher 1988), page 13.

[46] St Mary Bishophill Junior parish records, 12 August 1785.

[47] *Yorkshire Gazette*, 17 April 1858, page 7.

[48] *York Courant*, 18 August 1806, page 2 carries an advertisement for Richard's new business. He was three months out of apprenticeship, yet still purchased his freedom in the following year.

[49] *York Courant,* 25 February 1811, page 3 and 1 April 1811, page 2.

[50] Public Record Office (PRO) RG9/3552, Folio 50, page 19.

[51] *York Herald*, 23 February 1850, page 5.

[52] BIHR, Will of Isaac Wood, Volume 178, folio 126, proved 21 March 1828.

[53] *Yorkshire Gazette*, 19 November 1853, page 4.

[54] *Yorkshire Gazette*, 26 November 1859, page 6.

[55] Frederic Boase, *Modern English Biography* (1912, republished 1965 by Cass & Co Ltd, London), Volume 5, column 515.

[56] *Whitby Gazette*, 2 January 1891 gives a biography of Walter Grimshaw and a detailed account of the inquest.

[57] PRO RG10/4751, Folio 14, page 17.

[58] PRO HO107/2355 Folio 271, page 15.

[59] International Genealogical Index of the Church of Jesus Christ of Latter-Day Saints (1992).

[60] *Yorkshire Gazette*, 30 November 1907, page 7.

[61] Monumental Inscription in York Cemetery, D/22/40, transcribed by City of York & District Family History Society.

[62] *Yorkshire Gazette*, 23 September 1871, page 6.

[63] Baptism Register of St Crux, 21 April 1880.

[64] Slater, *Directory of Yorkshire* (1887), York section, page 49.

[65] Slater, *Directory of Yorkshire* (1887), York section, page 16.

[66] *Yorkshire Gazette*, 19 January 1828, page 2.

[67] W J Cook & Co, *York & District Directory* (1893), pages 290 and 218.

[68] *Yorkshire Gazette*, 1 February 1908, page 9.

[69] A G Watson (comp & ed), *York City Year Book and Business Directory - Volume 2* (1921), page 236 holds the most recent listing for the pawnbroker's business at Lady Peckett's Yard.

[70] Kelly, *Directory of the City of York & Neighbourhood* (1955), page 201.

[71] *Yorkshire Evening Press*, 24 & 30 May 1968 page 1, 3 September 1968, page 7.

[72] *Yorkshire Evening Press*, 5 November 1986, page 3.

[73] Charles Brunton Knight, *A History of the City of York* (Herald Printing Works 1944), page 583.

[74] Mrs Edwin Gray, *Papers and Diaries of a York Family 1764 – 1839* (The Sheldon Press 1927), page 56.

Y